TITCH

TITCH

A NOVEL BY

Chaim Bermant

ST. MARTIN'S PRESS
New York

 For information, address St. Martin's Press, 175 Fifth Avenue, New York, N.Y. 10010.

Library of Congress Cataloging-in-Publication Data

Bermant, Chaim, 1929–
Titch.

I. Title.
PR6052.E63T58 1987 823'.914 87-16146
ISBN 0-312-01099-0

First published in Great Britain by George Weidenfeld & Nicolson Limited.

First U.S. Edition

10 9 8 7 6 5 4 3 2 1

PROLOGUE

The day I left school in July 1939, I volunteered to join the army, but was turned down. Three years later I was conscripted, and when I asked the Medical Officer why I had been turned down the first time, he said: 'Didn't you know? Poor eyesight.'

'But my eyesight hasn't improved?'

'No, but the war situation has deteriorated.'

I was then sent off for basic training and, although not the most soldierly of soldiers, I acquitted myself fairly well and was given the impression that I would be sent on an officers' training course. 'Don't bank on it,' one friend told me, 'they're not all that free with pips.' 'The whole thing's a bloody lottery,' said another. Nothing, and no one, however, prepared me for what actually happened: I was sent to the *Polish* army.

'There must be some mistake,' I said.

'There's none.'

'But why the *Polish* army?'

'Because you're a fucking Pole, that's why.'

CHAPTER ONE

I was born in Poland in 1921 and moved with my family to Manchester in 1925 and have no recollection of my birthplace whatever. By the time I started school a year or so later, I had picked up sufficient English to pass as a native, at least in my own eyes, and thought I was accepted as such by others. It was not that I was ashamed of being Polish, but that I had an aversion to being different.

I was aware that my parents were also making desperate efforts to turn native. Both went to evening classes to learn English. Both insisted that I address them only in English, and both tried to speak only in English when I was around, with the result that until I was about six we were virtually incommunicado. To an extent we still are, and I am uncertain whether it is all due to those early years, or to an inherent inability to communicate.

I had a younger sister Soshana (who was known as such only to father, everybody else called her Sosh), who picked up a cold about the time we arrived in Manchester, and seemed to have picked up English about the same time and possibly by the same means, for I do not recall talking to her in any language other than English. I could nevertheless get rude reminders of my origins, and one of the rudest in my memory came one Friday afternoon.

We were seated in a large circle round our beloved teacher, Miss Pinkerton, who was telling us about the wonderful world in which we lived. 'There are hundreds of different countries,' she said, throwing out her arms, 'and hundreds of different people. Now Ling here, for example, is from China.' At which a slant-eyed little chap, with small pearly teeth, and an almost non-existent nose, smiled a bright little smile. 'And Farouq, here, is from India.' And a scrawny, dark-skinned lad with legs like match-sticks, and huge, black eyes, not only smiled, but stood up, clasped his hands under his nose, as if about to pray, then bowed. 'While Sammy,' she said, nodding towards me – and my heart stopped – 'is Polish.'

At which I almost cried. Had she said I was *from* Poland it mightn't have been so bad, but to say that I *was* Polish, was to question my very status as an Englishman. I quivered with indignation.

'Is there anything wrong Sammy?' asked Miss Pinkerton.

'I'm English,' I mumbled, tearfully.

'Of course you are, so is Ling, so is Farouq, we're all English, aren't we, children?'

'Yes Miss Pinkerton.'

But the damage was done. She had sown doubts about my innermost self.

As I have said, I had an aversion to being different, which I was to carry into early manhood and which could assume such acute forms that I came to call it 'contraphobia'. I was already different enough in being Jewish, but that, at least, was a difference which I shared with about half the class; I had no wish to be Polish as well. It was all right for the Lings and Farouqs to be Chinese or Indian, or whatever, because in the first place they weren't Jewish, and in the second, whether Jewish or not, they obviously looked different, whereas I thought I looked much the same as everybody else. I also feared it might affect my place in the affections of Miss Pinkerton, a large woman, with a large bosom and soft brown eyes.

When I taxed my father about it, he said: 'So all right, you were born in Poland, but you were only a baby when you left. What business is it of hers where you were born and when you came? It's not as if you've even got an accent. The woman's an anti-semite.'

Of all the words which floated my way during my early years, I suppose anti-semite was about the most common, but it was used so indiscriminately that for a long time I didn't know what it meant.

The milkman, for example, was an anti-semite because the clatter of his bottles woke father in the early hours. The postman was an anti-semite because he only brought bills. The bank manager was an anti-semite because he wouldn't extend credit. The gas-meter reader was an anti-semite because – or so father insisted – he made faulty readings, none of them in our favour. The dustmen were anti-semite because they left our dustbins half full. The road-sweeper was an anti-semite because – father alleged – he left our part of the road unswept. Even Mrs Sussman next door was an anti-semite because she complained about my father's noise, and when I pointed out that Mrs Sussman was herself Jewish, he said Jews were the worst anti-semites of all.

I was a precocious child and even at six realized that certain facts, no matter how unwelcome, were irreversible. I was not all that happy about being Jewish, but at least it had its compensations, whereas being Polish only seemed to carry handicaps; but if I was a Pole I felt I had the right to know more about Poland.

'Why this sudden interest?' said father. 'Are you doing it in geography or something? It's not even in the British Empire.'

'I want to know.'

'There's better things to learn about.'

'Why did you leave Poland?'

'Why don't you tell him?' said mother.

'Because of you, if you must know,' said father.

'But why me?'

'Because there was no future for you there, and there is here,' he roared.

'What are you shouting for?' asked mother. 'He's asking a perfectly reasonable question. Why don't you begin at the beginning?'

Father sighed the deep sigh of one who knows he's dealing with imbeciles, but can't do anything about it.

'It was very difficult in Poland, very difficult. Hard to make a living, hard to do anything. Anti-semites everywhere. You've got them here too, but in Manchester you also get decent yoks. In Poland you only got anti-semites.'

Father was a large, hefty, overbearing man, with wavy grey hair on his head and wiry little tufts sprouting in and around his ears, his nostrils and on the backs of his hands, and a nose of such noble proportions that it was not so much a feature among others, as a centrepiece. When he sneezed, one dived for cover. He had a manner and voice to go with his build, though mother (who had an excuse for everyone and everything) said that he had acquired his noisy ways because his mother was hard-of-hearing and his father was stone-deaf. He, for his part, was hard-of-listening. In Poland he was known as the Cossack.

Mother was small, slight, breathless and retiring, with straight, jet-black hair and a complexion like porcelain. She wore large glasses which made her look slightly owlish, and which sometimes slid from their place, because she had insufficient nose to restrain them. In Poland she had been known as the Chinawoman. She was as quiet as father was boisterous, but her authority was out of all proportion to her size, or, indeed, her sound, for she could silence father with a glance, and if that did not suffice, she only had to say: 'Now that's enough, Nathan', and father would dry up in mid-sentence. But she used her authority sparingly, perhaps too sparingly, and casual visitors came away with the belief that here was the typical silent, downtrodden, long-suffering little woman. She was more intelligent and less impulsive than father, but perhaps her main source of authority lay in the fact that she was of better family, and father was a great respecter of pedigree.

There was a third adult member of the family in the person of Aunt Malka, father's younger sister, a large, silent woman, with large lustreless eyes who, for all her size, moved about the place like a shadow so that one was barely aware of her presence. She referred to father as 'the Horse', and he called her 'the Cow', but at this stage of her existence (she was to undergo a dramatic transformation later) they never quarrelled, and I half-presumed the names were meant to be affectionate.

I took after mother in build, while my sister took after father in both build and temperament, and although a year my junior, she bullied me like an older sister and called me 'Titch' when she was in a good mood, or 'the Midget', when she was in a bad one (which she generally was).

There were quite a number of recent immigrants in Manchester at the time, but father built up a small import business in dairy produce and prospered more quickly than most of them, which does not mean he was rich, but he was solvent, which was more than could be said of the others. What was perhaps more to the point, he learnt English more quickly, and what with his rolled umbrella and bowler hat he was regarded among newcomers – and certainly liked to regard himself – as an English gentleman, all of which made him a person of some standing in our local synagogue. He was not a particularly religious man, but he liked to exercise authority and the synagogue was about the only place where he could do so, and not long after settling in Manchester he became lay head of the congregation.

The congregation was small and impoverished and its religious offices were conducted by laymen, and father put it to them that they would never get anywhere unless they found a Rabbi. What was perhaps more to the point, Aunt Malka had grown to an age (indeed, she was in danger of passing it) when she needed a husband, and father knew a man with the talents requisite for both.

'A marvellous young man,' he said. 'Good head, good family, pious, learned,' at which the treasurer of the congregation, a tailor called Fishel Krieger, asked: 'Does he speak a gut Engils?'

'Better than you,' said father.

'I don't have to speak Engils, I don't have to speak at all, but then I'm not a Rabbi. Does he speak a gut Engils?'

'He'll learn, in fact he's learning right now.'

'And supposing he doesn't?'

'Then he'll have to go.'

'And who's going to make him? It's more difficult to get rid of a bad Rabbi than a bad wife.'

'If he doesn't learn English in twelve months, he goes,' said father. 'You will have it all in writing.'

'Can't he come just for a trial?'

'Did you marry your wife just for a trial?'

'No, but I could see what a bargain I was getting. You're trying to sell us a pig in a poke. Where does he live?'

'In Poland.'

'You mean we'll have to pay his fares?'

'So what do you expect him to do? Walk?'

In the end father had his way, as he always did, by threatening that if they wouldn't have his man they would not only have to start looking for another Rabbi, but another president.

The young man eventually arrived and he didn't look all that young, nor did he look much of a Rabbi and with his red, pock-marked, sweaty complexion, deep-set blue eyes, heavy build and huge hands, he was more like an all-in wrestler. He did, however, have a beard, which grew in a fluffy crescent under his chin rather than on it, and looked like a muffler.

Father was careful to secure his services as a brother-in-law before he signed his contract as a Rabbi and we celebrated the engagement in our house.

He was not at all what I expected. I am not even sure that he was what Malka expected and neither of them exchanged as much as a glance during the entire evening, but he was formally installed as Rabbi the following week and a month later they were married and moved into a small terrace house a few streets from the synagogue.

One of course heard suggestions that father had sold them the Rabbi because he needed a brother-in-law, which may, indeed, have been the case, but they were not displeased with him. Most of them were small, slight and stunted, and they were impressed with his very bulk. He also led the services in a pleasant singing voice, and finally, he made strenuous efforts to learn English, and delivered a sermon in an English of sorts within three months of arrival. It was not the sort which would have been recognized as such by anyone familiar with the language, but it impressed most of his congregants and his praises were sung throughout Manchester.

His troubles were twofold. He had picked up a few stock expressions like 'fly in the ointment', 'flea in his ear', and 'nigger in the wood-pile', which he liked to use in every possible context, and a few impossible ones, and sometimes had niggers in the ointment and flies in the wood-pile. Moreover, he had arrived with a smattering of English derived mainly from his reading of the King James Bible and he would come out with phrases like, 'and they went thence out of Konstontyn, which is by way of Plotsk.'

I was ten by then and was spoken of, by father at least, as a child prodigy, and when I put it to him that the Rabbi's use of English was eccentric, he retorted: 'It's good enough for them.'

'But if no one will correct him, he'll never learn.'

'All right then, my professor, you can correct him,' and I was accordingly deputed to teach him English.

It wasn't easy, for I had to unteach him everything he had learnt, but he was a willing and intelligent pupil and within six months he knew enough to continue on his own. By then, however, a close friendship had formed between us and I continued to see him two or three times a week long after he had any need of my tuition.

Every Rabbi has a honeymoon period with his congregation which may last anything from a few months to a few years. With Holtzhacker, as our Rabbi was called, it lasted exactly a year for within that time he had acquired not only a working knowledge of English but a daughter and he sought to mark his twin accomplishments by asking for a rise.

To Krieger, the request smacked not only of presumption, but ingratitude. 'His Engils may be goot, but it's not that goot,' he said.

It was also whispered that he had wayward habits and the look of a drinking man. I didn't know what a drinking man was meant to look like, but he smelt like Finnegan, the synagogue caretaker who was a drinking man, and not infrequently drunk, and as our friendship ripened he offered me an occasional swig from a silver flask he carried in his breast pocket.

As the debate over Holtzhacker's salary continued, the congregation divided between pro- and anti-Rabbi factions, with the former led by my father and the latter by Krieger and what came into question was not only the Rabbi's salary, but my father's supremacy, for he was by then not the only English-speaking member of the congregation, nor the only solvent congregant, but *I* finally saved the day by winning a scholarship to Manchester Grammar School.

Once a boy passed his tenth year, the word 'grammar' was on everyone's lips. Not everyone knew what it meant, but it was regarded as a sort of password to a higher plane of attainment, and if a place in any grammar school was a half-way house to the Kingdom of Heaven, Manchester Grammar was the Kingdom of Heaven itself.

It was an achievement for any boy to win a scholarship to such a school, but it was almost unheard of for an immigrant to do so. There was an article about me in the local Jewish paper and a paragraph (with photo) in the *Manchester Evening News*. Both, I thought, harped excessively on my foreign origins, but I became something of a celebrity and people pointed me out in the street, and on trams, which I found rather pleasing, though I tried not to let it got to my head.

Father's stock, of course, rose immediately, and when I made a dramatic entry in synagogue in the celebrated striped cap and crested blazer, all prayer, and even all conversation stopped. As Holtzhacker put it later: 'If the Messiah should come, he'll have to come in a crested blazer, otherwise they won't give him a second look.'

Krieger withdrew (to fight another day); Holtzhacker got his rise; father was made Hon. Life President, and no sooner was he confirmed in the supreme dignity than he began to feel that he was too supreme a dignity to continue with the same congregation.

'I think we should move,' he said.

'Move?' said mother. 'What for?'

'What for? What have I got to do with all these old, broken-down tailors and cobblers and nobodies? We should move to a district where they have a better class of people.'

'We can't afford it.'

'Business is picking up.'

'But who says it'll stay up?'

My achievement, of course, raised me in the esteem of Holtzhacker. He had always treated me as an adult rather than a child, which was one of the reasons why I was drawn to him, but he now began to treat me as a confidant.

'There's no one to speak to in the synagogue,' he said, 'no one. A lot of ignoramuses and blockheads, but I suppose it's being stupid that keeps them religious,' which struck me as a strange thought coming from a Rabbi, and he added: 'I know you're not stupid, but you're still a young boy. You've got plenty of time to grow out of it.'

I mentioned that father had been talking about moving to another part of town.

'Moving? What for? Are the people round here not good enough for him?'

'You just said yourself they were stupid and ignorant.'

'For you and me maybe, but for your father? He's a good man, and a generous man, but an aristocrat he's not. Does he ever talk about his family?'

'Never.'

'I'm not surprised, but if he doesn't want to tell you, I can't tell you either.'

But he told me all the same.

'His mother was an ignorant washer-woman, a kindly old soul, but with not much up there, and too much down there, if you know what I mean. But his father? A brigand. Worse than a brigand. A brigand, at least, has to have a bit of courage, to go out on horseback, fire a gun maybe, and there's always the chance that he'll be caught and hanged. No, your grandfather was in business with brigands, and a low class of brigand at that, horse-thieves, smugglers, counterfeiters, forgers, anything which came his way, but he didn't try to raise his son in the family business. Your father's made something of himself, I will say that for him, but he'd have been nothing without your mother. Now her family was something. Doesn't she ever talk about them?'

'Hardly ever.'

'I suppose she's afraid that if she starts talking about her family, you'll start asking questions about his. She was a Corb, and where I come from the Corbs was the royal family. Your father and I were students together in Yeshiva. They couldn't afford to feed us and we ate different days with different families – a piece of herring here, a few potatoes there, and maybe a crust of bread, but with the Corbs we had white bread, fish, meat – on weekdays! And whole pieces of meat, and not stringy little bits like loose strands of hair, it was like a wedding. Old Corb had many sons, but only this one little daughter, born in his old age, the apple of his eye, though she didn't look his. He was large and fat, his wife was small and fat, and they had this thin little thing. She wasn't much to look at, and there was very little to grasp, but anyone who could get her as a wife was set up for life. At least that's what we all thought, and that's what your father thought, but it didn't work out that way because Corb's seven sons were all in the business and they didn't need another partner, especially as it was all going downhill. This was just after the war, Poland became independent and the Poles began boycotting Jewish shops and it was difficult even for a Corb to make a living, but a Corb doing badly was still better off than anybody else doing well. They gave him a few zlotys to start up on his own, and he wasn't doing too badly when they decided to pull up and leave. It was her idea. Everyone thought they were mad. You don't need much foresight to move when you're being chased, or when everything's falling about your ears, but to move when things are picking up takes a bit of doing. He sold out to his in-laws and came here, began again from the beginning and, as you see, he's not doing too badly, and he's even doing it honestly, but he would be nowhere without your mother. He may not have much brains, but what he hasn't in brains he makes up for in mazel. He didn't deserve a wife like your mother, and he doesn't deserve a son like you, but he shouldn't start thinking that just because the heavens have been smiling on him that he's the Lord's anointed, because I can also tell you that everything I've told you isn't everything I know.'

At which I stood by for more, but he must have felt that he had already said too much, for he quickly added: 'You mustn't believe everything I tell you, not because it's all lies, heaven forbid, but I'm only human and I can be envious. I was also a young man once, younger than your father, from better family – which everyone was – with a better head and a better education, and I was also slimmer and better looking, but I did nothing with myself.'

'Isn't being a Rabbi something?'

'A Rabbi? I was never a Rabbi. I was trained to be a Rabbi, which is not the same thing, because where I came from you couldn't train to be anything else. No, I did a bit of this and a bit of that, but nothing I did ever came to anything, and I wrote to your father to ask if he could do anything for me. He could, he said, if I became a Rabbi, so I became a Rabbi. If he had asked me to become a juggler, I would have become a juggler, and I would probably have enjoyed it more.'

One Saturday he invited me home for lunch. In spite of his revelations, I still had sufficient respect for his holy office to treat his invitation as a command, but I approached the occasion with dread. My mother was a particularly good cook, while Malka was a particularly bad one, for even when she served up pickled herring it was devoid of all piquancy, and she must either have perfected some sort of taste extractor, or something of her bland personality invaded her food.

She sat at table with her large placid eyes, not saying a word. Her husband was at pains not to turn his head in her direction and when he couldn't avoid doing so, something like despair spread over his face.

He drank a lot. His face reddened and became misty and after a time it began to emit actual smoke, as if he was burning internally, which in a sense he was and he again complained of his misfortune in having to pander to people he regarded with contempt.

'If your father is king round here, you can imagine what the rest are like.'

'Have you tried getting a job in London?'

'Doing what?'

'What you're doing here.'

'A Rabbi in London? Here among the tailors and cobblers they think I'm somebody, in London they would find me out.'

He was not generous in his estimates of his fellow men at the best of times, but in his cups he turned mainly upon himself, though whether drunk or sober he could be embarrassing in his estimates of me.

'One day,' he said, 'they'll have a plaque on this chair, "Sammy Hoch sat here." They'll have a plaque on your house, "Sammy Hoch lived here." A plaque on the synagogue, "Sammy Hoch prayed here." A plaque, if you'll excuse me, on your chamber-pot, "Sammy Hoch pissed here." You'll go to University, you'll be a great Professor, and when at the end of my days they will ask me what right have I to a place in heaven, I will say I knew Sammy Hoch, yea he was a guest at my table, they will wave me right in and give me a seat at the right hand of God.'

What was a particular source of wonder to him was the fact that I continued to attend synagogue at all. There were other Jewish boys in Manchester Grammar School, but they – and, indeed, their families – tended to treat their admission as a form of absolution from further Jewish observance. They stopped eating kosher, attending synagogue, or even mixing with other Jews. They had, so to speak, done their bit for the Almighty by securing a place among the Elect, and yet here was I in my striped cap and crested blazer, both proclaiming my election and yet continuing to behave as if I was but another schoolboy; he once said to me: 'I don't know why you bother, a boy like you.'

My conformity to Jewish observances arose mainly out of the fact that I had always conformed to them and they seemed the natural thing to do, and because they gave me a certain amount of pleasure. I liked the musty, dusty ambiance of the synagogue, the creaking floor, the rickety seats, the heavy, velvet, thickly embroidered curtain over the ark, the crudely carved lions on top of it, and the prayer for the Royal Family painted on the wall alongside it:

> May he who giveth salvation unto kings and dominion unto princes,
> whose kingdom is an everlasting kingdom, bless:
> Our Sovereign Lord King George.
> The Gracious Queen Mary,
> Edward, Prince of Wales,
> and all the Royal Family...

I even liked the old men with the furrowed brows and floppy whiskers, smelling of garlic and snuff.

My religious conformity certainly did not arise out of parental pressure, for my father, Life President though he was, rarely covered his head, did not always eat kosher, and, if pressure of business demanded it, as it sometimes did, would desecrate the Sabbath. Mother was rather more religious, but I noticed that on holiday they dropped almost all observances, as if, once away from home, they felt entitled to a holiday from the Lord.

Father in fact often grumbled about the amount of time I spent in synagogue. 'Do you want to become a Rabbi or something, God forbid,' he said more than once, nor was he happy about my friendship with Holtzhacker.

To father the world was divided into two: those who had made it, or who looked as if they might make it, and those who hadn't and wouldn't, and the very fact that Holtzhacker was dependent, directly, or indirectly upon his largesse, placed him irrevocably among the latter. He was, to use an expression often on father's lips, a *nebbich*, and the less one had to do with such people, the better.

In my eyes, at least, Holtzhacker was anything but a *nebbich*, for the expression conjured up someone small, wispy and helpless, which did not quite go with his build or personality. A few months later, however, I was to meet the real thing.

There was a Yiddish saying which father liked to quote, that one man's poor relative was another man's rich one, or vice versa. We had remote relatives called Rodgers who had helped father find his feet in Manchester and hardly had he attained a modicum of prosperity before he found poor relatives (or rather, they found him) in Poland who needed his help. And not only relatives, but friends, and friends of relatives and relatives of friends.

'They must think I'm Rothschild,' said father, and it brought to mind another saying that no man knows how many relatives and friends he has until he's made a bit of money.

They all wanted loans, some to get to America, some to South Africa, the Argentine, or even China. No one, to father's relief, sought a foothold in Britain, till one day he received a letter from a second cousin called Boyarski. It was, for a letter of that sort, surprisingly brief and to the point:

Dear Nathan,

I've been hearing wonderful things about you. I wish I could tell you wonderful things about me, but first I must start with my blessings. I have a wonderful wife Breine, a real mother in Israel, and three beautiful boys, bless them, Berale, Yankale and Fishale, but otherwise things aren't so good. Do you remember the big business my father-in-law used to have? Well, it wasn't so big, and it wasn't much of a business, and what there was of it has gone to pieces, and so has my father-in-law, poor man. Do you think there might be anything for me in England? And if there is, would you be able to lend me the money for a ticket? You would of course have it back the minute I earned it.

Your loving cousin,

Pesach Boyarski.

The letter was fortunately timed, for it arrived shortly after I won my scholarship and in a spasm of thanksgiving, father sent him the fare money and immediately busied himself to find him a job.

As always when faced with someone otherwise unemployable, father turned to religion and found him work as a sort of ecclesiastical odd-job man, conducting a service here, officiating at a funeral there, collecting synagogue subscriptions, and preparing boys for their Barmitzvah.

'It won't make you rich,' wrote father, 'but you won't go hungry.'

The job, however, was not in Manchester, but in a place as remote from it as possible, which in this instance happened to be Glasgow, in keeping with Nathan's law that if one rubbed shoulders with *nebbichs*, one became a *nebbich* oneself.

Boyarski was delighted with the opening. His original intention had been to come out on his own to earn enough money to bring his family over, but father lent them enough to come en bloc and they stopped over with us on the way north.

I vacated my bedroom for the parents and bedded down in the front room with the boys, aged seven, five and three. (The gaps, I learnt later, were due not to family planning, but to miscarriages and still-births.)

The mother was short and dumpy with a red face, bad teeth and a wig like an ill-kempt doormat. The boys were thin, not with the spare build of the non-fat, but the slight, shrunken frames of the under-nourished, and the father, lean and round-shouldered was half hidden behind a cataract of hair, which began on his cheek-bones, continued in an unbroken torrent over his mouth, and diverged at the chin to form two distinct tributaries which continued down to his chest. His very eyebrows were so shaggy as to look like upturned beards and his eyes shone out at the world like an owl trapped in a thicket.

Both he and his wife talked in a rapid, unintelligible Yiddish, he deep-voiced, she high-pitched and plaintive, while the boys sat huddled together with brooding eyes and running noses, snuffling in unison and saying never a word. They only came alive at the sight of food, on which they descended with shrill whoops like jackals on a carcase. Sosh took one look at them and fled.

They arrived on a warm day dressed for a Polish winter in clothes which were not only heavy and outlandish, but which seemed ready to fall apart. At the insistence of mother they stayed an extra day and she took the boys out, bought them shorts, shirts and sandals, and when they returned their own parents almost failed to recognize them.

When they left the next morning Sosh rushed from room to room, throwing open windows, as if to let out the stale smell of poverty.

Father, mother and I saw them off at the station and as the train pulled out father turned to us and said: 'What'll happen at the Barmitzvah?'

My Barmitzvah was still eighteen months away and father had already expressed anxieties how people like the Rodgers would mix with people like us, but now he began to worry how people like us would mix with people like the Boyarskis? How would he accommodate three such distinct worlds at the same event?

The Rodgers family consisted of Alfred and Theresa, and their two children Pippa and Edwin. Theresa's step-mother was my father's aunt, which made our relationship tenuous in the extreme and we would hardly have thought of them as relatives at all had they not been very helpful and very rich, and we referred to Alfred as uncle, Theresa as aunt, and their two children as cousins.

Theresa was a striking woman, tall and thin, with sunken cheeks, high cheek-bones, jet-black hair (which father said was dyed), and gleaming teeth (which father said were false). She was always heavily made up, and as father had a name for everybody, he called her, with his usual lack of originality, Jezebel. Alfred, a large, genial man, with a tentative little smile always hovering about his lips, he called the Ox. He also usually spoke of them as the Rogoznitzkys which, he said, was their real name. (That, at least, was something he had over them, for while names were being changed on every side, he had resolutely stuck to the name of Hoch, though I often wished he hadn't, for hardly anyone in school could pronounce it and I was generally known as Hooch.)

Given the fact that Alfred and Theresa had helped him to find his feet in Manchester, his hostility to them was surprising but, like Holtzhacker, he could never forgive those to whom he was beholden. It was a way of asserting his independence. It was also, in fact, rather contrived for he underwent a transformation in their presence. A toothy smile settled permanently on his face. His face softened and became deferential. He even lost something of his erect bearing, and seemed to shrink.

If we thought of them as kinsmen, I wasn't too sure how they considered us, but they did invite us to their home once a year, for Christmas dinner of all things.

Father always treated the invitation with a show of disdain.

'These people don't know if they're Jews or goyim. I don't know if we should bother to go,' but of course we always went and prepared for the occasion as if for a wedding. Mother had her hair done, Sosh wore a new frock, and father wore the black jacket, striped trousers and spats, his panoply of office as Life President of the synagogue. And we always came by taxi, as if public transport was unfitting for an occasion so grand.

And it was a grand occasion with twenty or more guests ranged round a vast table, with six gleaming pieces of cutlery by each plate, so that we were always a little at a loss as to what to use when. We had the usual fare, but in ample portions and beautifully served by liveried servants.

After the meal the old went into one room and the young into another, and although there were Christmas presents to be had from a Christmas tree, it was a moment I hated. Everybody knew everybody else and had lots of stories to exchange. The only person I really knew was my sister, and she didn't want to know me when we were in company.

Each year Edwin would come up dutifully to me, and each year we would have the same exchange.

'Oh hullo Sammy, still at school?' which, given my age, struck me as a daft question, but I always answered politely: 'Yes I am.'

'Like it?'

'Yes I do.'

'Gosh, do you? I positively hate school.'

My conversation with Pippa was along much the same lines, and of about the same duration, except that she never addressed me by name, presumably because she never remembered it. And then both, having done their duty, left me to my own devices, and I examined the presents and the baubles and lights on the Christmas tree, the titles of the books on the bookshelves, the labels on the gramophone records, traced the patterns on the carpet, and finally, though it was dark by then, I looked out of the windows on to the back garden. And thus one year when father made his usual show of not wanting to go, I asked him why we had to go if he didn't want to. He looked at me nonplussed.

'What else can you do on Christmas day?'

I suppose I came to dread the event not so much because of the boredom which followed the meal, but the condescending manner with which I was treated. Pippa and Edwin were only a year or two older than me, but they were both tall for their age, whereas I, if anything, was small for mine, and Edwin in particular would tower over me, hands in his jacket pockets, head thrown back, and address me like a landlord might address his tenantry. They made me feel that I not only belonged to a different class (which I readily accepted) but to a different generation.

All that, however, changed when I won the scholarship, and shortly after an item (with photograph) appeared about me in a local paper, we were invited to afternoon tea.

It was a blazing hot Sunday afternoon and although I had not yet started school, I was already wearing my cap and blazer, both of them several sizes too large, my mother having reckoned that as I was still growing (which I was, but very slowly) the right size would soon be too small, and the sweat poured down me in rivulets.

I was prevailed upon to remove my cap, but I was afraid (as I suspect were my parents) that if I removed my blazer, the aura of success which it gave me would vanish with it.

There were no other guests, Pippa and Edwin were away so that this was my first real encounter with the parents and I grew to like them both, especially the father.

He gave me a warm handshake and placed an arm round my shoulders.

'Well done, m'boy. We're all jolly proud of you. Good to have someone bright in the family.' I caught father's eye at that moment and, though his face was in the shadow, it glowed as if it was in the sun.

'I got a special letter from his headmaster to congratulate me,' he said.

'You should see the letters I get from Edwin's headmaster. Spend a fortune on his education. Never learns a thing.' He spoke quickly, in little spurts, with a slight stutter, which gave him a mildly diffident air.

'Pippa's much worse,' said his wife.

'Pippa's very bright, but spoilt. Never opens a book, but Edwin's a bit dim, I'm afraid.'

'Takes after his father,' said the wife.

We were sitting in deck-chairs with leg-rests and my aunt was wearing a silk, sleeveless frock. It occurred to me that I had never seen her in the summer before, and she looked a different person. She was deeply tanned, without a trace of make-up. Her hair was cut shorter, with stray strands playing about her eyes in the breeze. She used to bare her teeth by way of a smile, but now she radiated warmth without even moving her lips, and a quality of tenderness which I had not previously associated with her, but the thing I most remember about that afternoon was the sight of her long, slender, deeply tanned, legs.

I daresay I must have seen legs before, only I hadn't noticed them and they had certainly not occurred to me as being an attractive part of a woman's body. I could not take my eyes off them, and from then on I counted the days till the Christmas dinner in the hope that I might get a glimpse of them again.

Came Christmas, however, and she was back to her old,

gaunt, painted self, and in a long dress to boot, but for the first time I felt (as, I think, did my parents) that we were invited not as a good cause, but because they wanted our company and when, after the meal, the different generations dispersed to their different rooms, even my sister showed an awareness of my presence.

Edwin came over to congratulate me on the scholarship, but otherwise kept his distance, and it seemed to me that whereas he had previously felt that I wasn't in his class, he now felt that he wasn't in mine.

Pippa was rather less overawed at my success.

'Daddy doesn't stop talking about you,' she said. 'If he's going to go on like that, we're all going to hate you.'

I was cheered by that. It was recognition of sorts and even if I was still left to myself I no longer felt I was ignored and even derived a certain smug satisfaction from my own company. I was, of course, not in my school blazer and was wearing a brand-new suit with my first pair of long trousers, but I had by now attended a full term at Manchester Grammar and the feeling of reassurance which the blazer had offered, was now built into me.

But in any case I felt sufficiently preoccupied in beholding Pippa, if only from a distance – her fair hair, her long neck, her beautiful shape – and catching stray snatches of her languorous voice. I imagined I was in love with her.

Though precocious in some respects, I was retarded in others and still thought of love in story-book terms, and even with the self-assurance which the scholarship had given me, and the high place I enjoyed in her father's esteem, I regarded her as a distant unattainable goddess. And story book or not, she was distant and unattainable, being older than me, taller than me and, of course, infinitely richer than me.

Father was regarded in the synagogue as a local magnate, though we only had a three-bedroomed house with a small back-yard by way of a garden. We had no car, no maids and, until we had a geyser installed, we had no hot water, and about the only luxury I can associate with those days was my mother's silver fox fur.

That silver fox was a source of contention. Father brought it home in triumph one evening after a small business coup, and mother recoiled from it as if it might attack her.

'What'll I do with it?' she asked.

'Pickle it and serve it up with onions and gherkins,' said father ironically, but being a good, loyal wife, she wore it, at least on state occasions, which is one of the reasons why she loathed state occasions, for she felt and looked odd in it, and was half-asphyxiated by it, but father cherished the sight of it as proof of his prosperity, until, glancing up at the lady's gallery the following Yom Kippur he found the entire front row packed with silver foxes. It had become to the women what the prayer-shawl was to the men.

Father, to use his own expression, was in fact only 'comfortable', and not very comfortable at that, and if he was thought rich it was mainly because he was generous.

The Rodgers, however, really were rich, not merely in the sense that they had more money, but they looked different, spoke differently, dressed differently and even smelt differently, and seemed to live on a different plane of existence. My scholarship and that Sunday afternoon tea-party had brought us a little nearer, so that my father and Mr Rodgers were by now on Nathan and Alfred terms, but we could not yet contemplate the possibility of having them over to our house and, as I have said, father was even worried as to how they might fit into my Barmitzvah celebrations, and with the Boyarskis about, the matter became one of acute anxiety.

At first father toyed with the idea of having a two-tier affair, one for the posh guests, and the other for hoi polloi, or 'the tailors and the cobblers', as he called them, but mother wouldn't have it, and he comforted himself with the possibility that as the return fare from Glasgow to Manchester was rather expensive the Boyarskis would not be able to make it. No sooner were the invitations sent out, however, than they replied that they would be happy to come.

Although I had not said a word about it to anyone I too was a little apprehensive about their presence, for I could see them all arriving in their heavy boots and coarse threadbare outfits, Berale, Yankale and Fishale, outlandish beings with outlandish ways, and their father like a walking hedgerow, and their squat mother with her flushed face and her plaintive, high-pitched voice, and I feared that they might cramp my style.

Holtzhacker shared my feelings. He had prepared for the Barmitzvah as if it was his own wedding, had acquired a new suit and had prevailed upon the board of management of the synagogue to provide him with a new cap and gown. Father had told him of the important visitors who would be in synagogue for the occasion and he told me that he would be preparing a sermon which would continue to ring in my ears till the day I died. For once, he thought, he would have a congregation worthy of his talents. In the circumstances, the news that the Boyarskis too would be coming put a damper on his zeal.

'I don't know why your father has anything to do with them,' he said. 'I know them all, a family of horse-thieves. If they're in Glasgow let them stay in Glasgow; why have them at your Barmitzvah? Let's pray it should snow.'

He must have prayed hard, for snow it did, with a vengeance. The city and the surrounding shires were engulfed and father ceased worrying about the Boyarskis and started worrying about the Rodgers, for they lived on the outskirts of the city, in Cheshire, where the drifting had been particularly heavy. In the event, the Boyarskis – all five of them, with a sixth fast on the way – made it and the Rodgers did not.

The father came in shirt and tie and a well-cut suit with even his eyebrows trimmed, and his beard cut away to a fine point so that he looked like a younger and slimmer version of George V. Berale, Yankale and Fishale came likewise smartly attired and now answered to the names of Bernard, Jackie and Freddy, respectively. Where they had been wordless before, they now jabbered away like their father, but in English instead of Yiddish or, rather, in Scots, so that I found them almost equally unintelligible. Bernard, now nine, was an authority on the history and prospects of every football team in and around Glasgow and had claims to being a promising footballer in his own right. He was also good at school and, though four years my junior, he was almost my height. Where I had feared embarrassment, I was almost upstaged.

In the end I performed before a half-empty synagogue which became emptier as the morning progressed, for the heating, which functioned poorly at the best of times, broke down altogether and Holtzhacker gave his sermon at the double in an overcoat and muffler.

One Friday evening I was in synagogue. I had, as was my custom, come a few minutes early so that I could have a chat with Holtzhacker, but there was no sign of him, nor was he there by the time we were due to start and, as we were a man short of a quorum, we could not start without him.

We waited ten minutes, quarter of an hour, twenty minutes, and when he had still not turned up I was sent round to his house to see if anything was wrong.

Aunt Malka, in her Sabbath best, with a silk kerchief round her head, was surprised to see me. He had left for synagogue more than half an hour before and it was only a few minutes' walk.

My father, who did not normally attend synagogue on Friday night, was hurriedly summoned and – Sabbath or not – arrived by taxi.

Our first, and most obvious, thought was to call the police, but he wouldn't hear of it.

'If we call the police it'll be in all the papers. We don't want a scandal.'

'But we've already got one,' said Krieger.

'He could be in danger,' I chirped in. Father looked at me with displeasure, as if I had gone over to the enemy, but others took up my point, the service was converted into an extraordinary general meeting and by a vote of six to one, with three abstentions, it was decided to go to the police.

Householders on his route to synagogue were questioned. No one had seen him. Inquiries were made at hospitals, railway stations, bus stations, but no one could recall anyone answering to his description.

Malka was questioned at length. She seemed more bewildered than perturbed, but could not tell them anything. He had said nothing about leaving, nor left a note to indicate his plans, and he hadn't packed. All his clothes, other than those he wore, were in his wardrobe, and even his toothbrush was in its bracket by the bathroom sink.

The police asked if she could tell them anything about his friends. 'Friends?' she said. 'He had no friends. He's a

Rabbi.' Then someone mentioned that he liked to have a drink before setting off for synagogue. Perhaps he'd had a drink too many and fallen into the canal?

The canal was dragged but nothing was found. It was as if the earth had opened and swallowed him up.

CHAPTER TWO

I missed Holtzhacker and was pained by the fact that although he had frequently hinted at the possibility of flight, he had never told me, his friend and confidant, anything about his plans, so that his disappearance left me with a personal sense of betrayal. But that was as nothing compared to the feelings of his congregation.

'We took him from nowhere,' said Krieger, 'got him a house, made him a somebody. I even made him a new outfit at cost price, and look what he does, leaves his wife and child and runs off with another woman – on *Shabbos*!'

That he had fled on the Sabbath was an undoubted fact, that he had gone off with another woman was a matter of pure conjecture, but it was generally assumed that a man would not leave free accommodation and a steady job without good cause, and what better cause than another woman?

'You should be pleased,' said father, 'you didn't want him in the first place.'

'No, but now we're without a Rabbi, and we've still got the cost of paying for his house and supporting his family.'

Krieger, a widower, had lately remarried, and his second wife had private or, as someone put it, 'very private', means and within a matter of weeks he was transformed from mere tailor (and not much of one at that) to gents' outfitter and now he looked for a position in the synagogue in keeping with his new status. Holtzhacker's flight gave him one. An 'extraordinary, extraordinary', meeting of the congregation was called, and father, knowing that the sense of the meeting would go against him, spiked their guns by resigning all his offices, including that of Life President. And while he was at it, he resigned from the synagogue altogether and moved house.

'I should have done it years ago,' he said. 'What have I got to do with these *shleppers*?' but in fact he felt, and looked slightly diminished by the change.

We moved to a more fashionable part of town and he joined a more fashionable congregation, but while he had been king in the old synagogue, he was a nobody in the new one, and father did not take easily to being a nobody. Moreover, boys with striped caps and crested blazers were ten a penny in the new place, so that he couldn't even look to me to raise his status, and he became less frequent in his attendance, and even less observant in his religious duties, possibly in the belief that God now expected less of him.

The disappearance of Holtzhacker had not involved me in any crisis of faith because, as I have suggested, my religious observances had more to do with habit than belief, but Holtzhacker had been an important part of that habit. Moreover, the old synagogue had been a converted Methodist chapel, while the new one was large and purpose built in a style that drew its inspiration from the Odeon cinemas which were springing up all over the place. One half-expected the Rabbi to emerge from the depths on a Wurlitzer, and the whole ambiance was so different that I no longer felt compelled to attend services with any regularity, which father found reassuring. Instead, my sister discovered religion.

She had rarely set foot in the old synagogue, but then its ladies' gallery was full of musty old dears with tear-stained prayer-books and moth-eaten furs, whereas in the new it was more like a fashion parade, and when she appeared – inevitably towards the end of the service – every head, including that of the Rabbi and Cantor, swivelled in her direction. She was fifteen by then and fully grown, perhaps even – if truth be told – a little over-grown, but she was poised and self-assured and smartly dressed, and where I had been something of a celebrity in my own right, my sole claim to fame now was that I was my sister's brother.

She was still at school and I was startled by the weekly transformation from girlhood to womanhood, from gymslip, thick stockings and pudding-basin hat, to satins and silk stockings and high heels, and rouge and lipstick. She not only looked different and smelt different, she assumed a new personality and ceased to be the bullying sister and instead of referring to me as Titch, or the Midget, she called me by my actual name. I was not, however, sure if I welcomed the change, partly because I rarely welcomed changes, especially sudden ones, and partly because she tended to patronize me, and on the whole I would rather be bullied than patronized.

She also began to show an inquisitiveness into my private life which I resented, and I resented it principally because I had no private life to speak of.

'I never see you with a girl,' she said. 'You're sixteen already; aren't you interested in girls, or are you still pining for Holtzhacker?'

I had few friends of any sort, not because I was shunned, but because I was studious by nature and by and large I preferred the company of books to the company of people, or at least the sort of people to whose company I had access, and the nearest thing I had to a friend was Sol Krieger (a son of father's old enemy), who was by now also at Manchester Grammar, though as a common or garden fee-paying boy. He was tall, thin, and rather unprepossessing, with wire-rimmed glasses and buck teeth. He worked even harder than I did, never went out on weekdays or even Saturday nights. We would often go walking together on the moors on Sundays, but even then he would, so to speak, bring his studies with him, and he would ask me to test him on his knowledge of Virgil. He was not exciting company.

I would not in the least have minded going out with a girl, but girls seemed remote and inaccessible. There were, of course, none at school. My sister had countless friends, but never a girl among them, and our annual pilgrimages *chez* Rodgers had ceased because the family now wintered abroad, so that I even ceased to dream about Pippa.

Alfred Rodgers was in the metal industry and on a fairly large scale. Father often came across his name in the business columns of the papers and he would read out the details aloud, as if he had a share in his enterprise, but we seemed to have lost all contact with him or his family. Then one day, out of the blue, Sosh and I received an invitation to a party for Pippa at the Midland Hotel.

Father demanded to know why he and mother were not invited. 'Are they ashamed of us? Is my English not good enough for them? Does he think I haven't got a good suit? Send back the invitation.'

'Can't you see it's for young people?' said mother.

'And what am I? An ancient monument?'

The Midland was the best hotel in town and the venue for the grandest of grand Barmitzvahs and weddings, and he could not imagine that even the Rodgers would use it for an occasion so minor as a birthday party. This, however, was to be no ordinary party, but a coming-out ball. Dress was formal and I acquired my first dinner-suit. Sosh suggested – in all seriousness, I think – that I also get high-heeled shoes, 'like the Spaniards wear'.

'There's nothing wrong with being short,' said mother.

'Not while you're still growing, but I think he's stopped.'

'Look,' I said, 'if you think I'm going to cramp your style, I'll go on my own.'

'It's not that, but if you're going to dance with a girl, you want to look her in the eyes.'

But somehow in my new, beautifully cut dinner-suit I did not feel that my slight size would be a serious disadvantage.

The day I received the invitation I enrolled in a crash course in ballroom dancing. My teacher was a large middle-aged woman with a huge bosom and when she clasped me to her person, I lost sight of my bearings. It was a pleasant enough sensation – in fact I did my best to stay clasped – but it limited my mobility and as a result I never quite mastered the quick-step, the foxtrot, the tango, or even the waltz, but I did nevertheless manage to manoeuvre her round the floor with a certain amount of grace, and when Sosh and I got to the Midland, I felt ready to take the place by storm.

The moment I entered the ballroom, however, my determination vanished, for the first person I encountered was the tall, lordly figure called Safran, a particularly detested school prefect. A glance from him might have been sufficient to lift me out of my euphoria and my dinner-suit, but what was worse, he looked straight at me without the merest sign of recognition, suggesting that I, Samuel Jacob Hoch, scholarship boy and mathematical prodigy of the Upper Fifth, had never even impinged upon his reckoning.

There were over a hundred Jewish boys at the Manchester

Grammar School, and they could be divided into three main groups, Jewish Jews, common or garden Jews and crypto Jews. The second regarded the first as fanatics, the first regarded the second as goyim, the first and second regarded the third with contempt.

The fanatics (of whom I was one) were known as such because they did not play games on Saturdays and stayed off school on Jewish festivals. (They also, of course, did not have school on Christian festivals, so they had it every way.) The goyim were so called because they rarely conformed to any Jewish observance at all, though they made no attempt to hide their Jewishness and, in some cases, were proud of it. The cryptoes were boys who were, or whom we suspected of being, Jews, but who treated the fact as a dark secret.

We were in fact in two minds about the last mentioned, for if we were generally inclined to scorn them, we were perfectly prepared to take pride in their achievements, and any boy, not already known to be Jewish, who gained any particular distinction in class or on the field, was subjected to close scrutiny, usually in the shower-room.

Irrefutable evidence was hard to come by, but we did have certain ground rules so that, for example, if a boy excelled in maths we were inclined to presume he was one of us, unless he could show definite proof to the contrary, though if he excelled in athletics we presumed – unless we knew otherwise – that he was one of them.

The trouble with Safran was that he excelled in everything, and was both scholar and athlete. He was also, with his tall build and aristocratic bearing, a lord among men and looked the prefect long before he became one. We would have dearly loved to claim him as one of us but sadly concluded that if he was in fact a Jew he would have had the sense to realize that with his dark eyes, swarthy complexion, long nose and outlandish name, he could not have passed as anything else, and that if he had hoped to do so he would have changed both his name and his nose. In other words (which may show how the Jewish mind works) we felt he could not possibly be a Jew because he showed too many symptoms of Jewishness.

All of which, however, was almost beside the point, for he was almost universally regarded as Jewish by the rest of the school, and we basked in his glory while knowing, in our heart of hearts, that we were not entitled to do so.

Then one day a new boy to the school arrived with the news that he definitely was Jewish.

'My father does business with his father,' he said, 'and knows for a fact that they're Jews from Syria or Persia, or some place like that.' Which should have been good news, though we weren't sure how to take pride in the achievements of a Jew who was ashamed to be Jewish, and we regarded him with mixed feelings until the Cattle Pen incident.

The Cattle Pen was an area at the back of the gymnasium into which latecomers were herded until morning assembly was over. Normally our names would be taken, and the more persistent offenders suffered the usual penalties. One morning, however, Safran, who was by then Senior Prefect, decided to address us. 'I can't help noticing,' he began, 'that you people seem to take a pride in unpunctuality . . .' I heard nothing more. Certainly I remembered nothing more.

It was a known fact that most of the persistent latecomers (myself among them) were Jewish, and had the words been uttered by anyone else they would not have been taken amiss, but coming from him, they were a bit much.

I was speechless with rage and if I only had the courage I would have demanded: 'What do you mean by *you* people? Who the hell do you think *you* are?' but just then a voice behind me asked those very questions in those very words. I looked round. It was Krieger, his face white with anger.

We held our breath. To answer back any prefect was effrontery enough. To answer back Safran, and especially in such terms, was a form of lèse-majesté. Safran, for his part, remained entirely composed.

'What's your name, boy?'

'Krieger.'

'Will you be good enough to come to my room after I have finished.' We heard later that he was suspended for the rest of the term.

Krieger became the hero of the hour and I suggested that we raise the matter with the High Master, but Krieger didn't want it and as the term was, in any case, nearly over, we left it.

And now, only a matter of weeks later, on this night of nights, when about to be launched on a new life of gaiety, I found myself in the dark, brooding presence of the beast himself. I felt shaken and shrunk and the very lapels of my dinner-suit seemed to curl. And were it not for that suit, and the money I had spent on the dancing lessons, I might have walked out there and then.

I looked around for Sosh, but she was already caught up in the whirl, and I slouched around on my own till Pippa came over and asked me to dance, but not even the sight of her golden shoulders rising above her blue gown, her fair hair, her bright smile, was sufficient to ease my mood, especially as I was perfectly aware that she had only asked me to dance precisely because I was on my own. I had once again become a good cause. I forgot even the few steps I had picked up from my dancing-teacher and waltzed when I should have foxtrotted, and foxtrotted when I should have quickstepped.

'I'm sorry,' I said, 'I'm not a particularly good dancer.'

'You're a particularly bad one,' she said, 'but you're light on your feet so it's not too difficult to guide you around. Something's biting you, isn't it?'

'Biting?'

'You look as if you've found a shilling and lost half-a-crown.'

'Is that why you asked me to dance?'

'Yes, as a matter of fact.'

I found her frankness oddly comforting.

'I've had a bit of a shock,' I said.

'Bump into someone you'd rather not see? Happens to me all the time. An old flame?'

'It's far more complicated than that. See that tall chap with the wavy hair over there?'

'Snow-white you mean?'

'He's called Safran.'

'We've always called him Snow-white. They used to be neighbours.'

'Is he Jewish?'

'Is he what?'

'Jewish.'

'Does it matter? You know you're in danger of becoming

a Jewish bore, and I don't just mean a bore who happens to be Jewish – though God knows there are enough of those – but the sort of Jew who goes on about Jews and being Jewish and can't talk about anything else. Even father, whose family has lived here for generations and who has never had much to do with Jews, is beginning to get like that. I'm sick of the subject and can't understand how you're not. Can't you just relax and enjoy yourself? Look around you. The place is full of pretty girls. Why don't you grab hold of one and fuck her?'

With that she left me on my own in the middle of the floor, and I remained there speechless, arms in front of me like a petrified penguin, while the band played on, and might have remained there all night, had her father not come dancing over to me to thrust a drink into my hand.

He led me to a corner table. 'Come on, boy, you're old enough for a brandy, aren't you? Drink it up. It'll do you good.'

I drank it up and nearly choked.

'Difficult girl, Pippa. God knows what'll happen to her. Terribly spoilt. Her mother you see. Very hard life. Made things too easy for the children. Edwin's a duffer, but fairly decent sort. Pippa's bright, but fairly nasty. No telling what she might come out with. Awkward age, apart from anything else, though off-hand I can't recall an age when she wasn't awkward. Terribly sorry. Spend half my life apologizing for her. Always thought she meant well, but I'm not even sure about that...'

And so he continued to mumble on, more to himself than to me. I only listened with half an ear trying to digest what I'd heard, and not only the words but the fury behind them. She reminded me a little of Sosh, but I doubted if even Sosh would snarl the head off a guest at her own ball.

I suppose if I had had any self-respect I would have walked out, but I was not so much wounded as stunned, especially at those final words. Nowadays one can rarely pass a playgroup without hearing one toddler tell another to go and fuck himself, but this was in 1938, and at a society ball. Was this how society girls spoke? And did the advice she offered suggest the way they behaved? Or was it merely that I lived too sheltered a life? I felt that whatever happened, I would have to have another word with her before the night was out.

She must have felt the same, for a few minutes later, after I had fortified myself with another brandy (this time without mishap), she came over to me, looking a little contrite.

'You must be angry with me,' she said.

'Angry? No, not angry, a bit bewildered though, and perhaps a little bruised.'

'I'm sorry, I had no right to speak to you like that – I hardly know you.'

'Is that how you speak to people you do know?'

'I don't really know what got into me – but look, can we talk?'

'We are talking.'

'Not here, it's too noisy.'

We tried the bar but it was even noisier and we finally found a quiet spot of sorts in a small vestibule by the kitchen.

'Aren't you neglecting your guests?' I said.

'Bugger my guests, I didn't want this party in the first place.'

'You don't look the sort of person who could be talked into doing anything you didn't want – or talked out of anything you did.'

'How can you say that? You don't know me at all. I've been bullied into doing things I didn't want all my life. I never wanted to be sent away to a posh boarding school with sniffy girls and snooty mums, or to live in that huge house with servants and spongers and hangers-on, or spend winters on the Riviera surrounded by podgy gown-merchants and their vulgar wives, and I didn't want this fucking ball.'

'Is that how they speak at boarding-school?'

'I'm sorry, I don't normally go on like this, but I feel stifled.'

'And every time you say fuck, it's like a window opening somewhere.'

'You may laugh, but that's exactly how I feel. Father's convinced there's going to be another war. If there is, I'm going to join the army or navy, anything to get away from home. When I read the war poets at school I wondered why everyone rushed to the colours, now I understand.'

Her mother appeared just then, looking magnificent but harassed. She threw me an apologetic smile and turned to her daughter.

'Darling, you can't leave your guests on their own. Everybody's looking for you.'

'Mummy can't I just have a few minutes' peace? I'll be back soon.'

Her mother turned to me: 'You'll see that she does, won't you?'

'I'll deliver her in person,' I said.

When she was gone, Pippa said: 'I don't think she approved.'

'Of me, do you mean?'

'Not you so much, but of you taking up too much of my time. I'm eighteen, you see, nearly nineteen. There are about half a dozen hand-picked eligible young men here and she wants me to circulate among them. The rest are so much ballast.'

'And I'm part of the ballast.'

'In her eyes, not in mine.'

'That's very kind of you, but in the circumstances shouldn't I return you to the throng?'

'It can wait, unless you're bored with my company.'

'Bored? With your company? Just seeing you on Christmas Day used to be enough to carry me through the winter.'

'Oh God, those awful dinners, how I hated them – and you were such an odious little prig.'

'Is that how you saw me? I hardly opened my mouth.'

'It wasn't what you said, it was the way you looked. You were so full of yourself, the typical, cocky little Jewish swot.'

I was beginning to feel slightly uncomfortable.

'I promised your mother I would have you back in a minute,' I said.

'You can leave my mother to me.'

'But all those eligible, hand-picked young men?'

'Don't be sarcastic.'

'Is Safran one of them?'

'This is where we came in, isn't it? He is Jewish, seeing you asked – doesn't he look it?'

'He doesn't admit to it.'

'Why should he have to admit to it? Is it an offence of some sort?'

The cordiality had vanished from her voice. I had obviously touched upon a sore point, but it was too late to change the subject.

'You're obsessed with this Jewish thing, aren't you? It's getting to be the same with everybody – even father. I suppose we've got Hitler to thank for that.'

'Why do you say even father?'

'Because he never used to bother with these things, not that he was ashamed of being Jewish, and most of our neighbours and friends were Jews, but so what? It wasn't something he thought about or talked about. But now, whatever the topic of conversation, it always leads back to the fucking Jews, and I get bored with it.'

'I think I had better get you back to your hand-picked eligible young men before I cop it from your mother.'

'I'm sorry, I lost my temper again.'

'You're entitled to – you know me now.'

Her mother was upon us again and this time threw a dark look in my direction rather than an apology, and snatched her away.

I felt oddly bucked by that conversation even though it had ended in something like acrimony. I was too young, too poor and perhaps too short to be among the hand-picked eligibles, but we had established a definite rapport. The brandy had no doubt helped, but so had her obscenities. There's nothing like an expletive to bring a girl down to earth.

I returned to the ballroom with a new confidence, and ran into my sister.

'Where have you been all evening? I wanted to give you a dance.'

'You? Want to dance with me?'

'Mummy made me promise I would.'

I bowed low, took her hand and led her through a tango.

'Have you been drinking?' she asked.

'Why? Am I doing it wrong?'

'No, you're doing it beautifully, and you sound odd – jaunty.'

I couldn't continue the conversation, for when the music

stopped Edwin – Pippa's brother – pounced upon her. I looked round for Pippa and found her in close conversation with a tall, elegant young man with fair hair and a ginger moustache, presumably one of her mother's hand-picked eligibles, and took it that I had had as much of her company as I was likely to get that evening.

The band was playing a rhumba and Edwin, I noticed, was holding Sosh a good deal more closely than the dance rhythm called for. The place was crowded with pretty girls in magnificent gowns but she, possibly because of her height and her build, outshone them all.

I looked around for a likely partner and noticed a slight but well-formed little girl, with a snub nose and determined chin. There was something vaguely familiar about that nose and chin, and as soon as the music stopped I cut through the crowd and almost pounced on her.

'I was going to sit this one out,' she said.

'Can't we sit it out together?' I asked.

'If we must,' she said, without much enthusiasm. 'You're Sosh's brother, aren't you?'

'Is that my only claim to fame?'

'I met you years ago, at Pippa's. Christmas dinner, remember? – you've forgotten.'

'How could anyone forget?'

'You've forgotten me though. You used to keep yourself to yourself. I once asked Sosh who was that stand-offish little twerp, and she said, my brother.'

'That's the second compliment I've had this evening. Pippa called me a cocky little Jewish swot, and now I'm a stand-offish little twerp. I don't suppose it occurs to girls of your class that people can be shy.'

'Girls of my class? What sort of class do you think I belong to? Or Pippa, for that matter? My father, who was bog Irish, married Uncle Alfred's sister, that red-haired bit of goods over there with the long cigarette-holder. There's nothing to the family except money, though they made it the hard way – they married it.'

'Mr Rodgers didn't marry money.'

'Didn't he just, he did better than any of them. He got not only money but looks.'

'We can't be talking about the same people. Mrs Rodgers – Pippa's mother – comes from the same part of the world as my family, and she was absolutely penniless.'

'She may have arrived penniless, but she didn't remain penniless for long. She was the mistress of Uncle Alfred's biggest customer, and he left her a fortune. The family contested the will, it was in all the papers. Mummy still has the clippings, so don't you start talking to me about class. We're scum with money, and not all that much money at that.'

I'd often heard of inverted snobbery but had never come upon such a striking instance of it. I wanted to know more.

She complained of being hungry so we went to the buffet and I watched with disbelief as she stoked up her plate with enough salmon mayonnaise to feed a household.

'You must forgive me,' she said, 'I eat like a horse.' And she did and when she cleared one plate, we went back and I waited while she filled another.

'You mustn't think I'm greedy,' she said, 'but Mummy's never learnt to cook. She never even learnt how to keep a cook, and if it weren't for all these parties and balls I'd starve. Aren't you eating at all?'

'I'm not really hungry.'

I spent the next half hour by the buffet while she helped herself to successive helpings of fruit salad, chocolate mousse, icecream and a great chunk of schwartzwald torte.

The spectacle of so much going into so little was beginning to pall somewhat, but having discovered how to engage a girl in conversation, I had no idea how to disengage myself and I had visions of spending the rest of the evening watching her demolish what was left of the buffet. I could hear the sound of music, laughter and gaiety next door.

'Do you like Scottish country dancing?' I said.

'No,' she said, 'but if you do, don't let me stop you. I like to get the eating over and done with before the rush begins, and before mummy sees me. She says I embarrass her.'

We were joined by several other couples and I wasn't sure if she wasn't embarrassing me.

'Shouldn't you be mixing with hand-picked eligibles?' I asked.

'I should. Mummy'll he here in a minute demanding to know why I'm not dancing. You'll like her.'

'What makes you so sure I will?'

'Everybody I know does – all the men that is, that's why I'm still on the shelf. As soon as I get friendly with a chap, he goes for my mother. Sometimes they befriend me to get at my mother. It's very sad, really. When she was a girl it was the other way about. All her mother's boyfriends went for her. That's how she met daddy. He was grandma's chauffeur.'

Her mother swept in at that moment, a tall, elegant, exquisitely shaped woman with red hair and a rather hard face, who looked as if she might have been the proprietrix of a high-class brothel and who, without as much as a glance in my direction, turned upon her daughter.

'I thought I'd find you here. The way you stuff yourself one would think I never fed you.'

'You never do.' Which brought the conversation to an abrupt end. The mother flounced out of the room. The daughter continued to guzzle schwartzwald torte unconcernedly.

'She'll kill me when I get home tonight, but what she doesn't know is that I shan't be coming home tonight. I'm going on to another party, are you?'

'I'm afraid not.'

'You can come with me if you want.'

'How can I? I haven't been invited.'

'Do you never gatecrash?'

'No. Do you?'

'All the time. You know, I think I'm beginning to see what you mean by class. There are the free classes, and the restrained class, and you belong to the restrained class, don't you?'

A little later Mr Rodgers came bearing down upon us.

'I see you have absconded with my favourite niece,' he said to me.

'Has mummy sent you to retrieve me?' she demanded.

'Good heavens no, but I was hoping for the pleasure of a dance and you were nowhere to be seen.'

She popped a morsel of cake daintily into her mouth, licked her fingers, and waved me bye-bye.

'Enjoy yourself, young man,' said her uncle, 'party-time's nearly over.'

My status as a non-eligible, whether hand-picked or otherwise, had been doubly confirmed, but I was slightly relieved to be on my own again. I had found that little girl slightly overwhelming.

People now began to flood into the buffet, among them Sosh and Edwin.

'You on your own?' she said. 'I thought I saw you make off with Sue Molloy.'

'Is that her name?'

'Pippa's cousin, poisonous little thing.'

'Very clever,' said Edwin. 'Brains of the family.'

It was getting late and I asked Sosh what time she was planning to go home.

'I'm going on to a party,' she said, 'so don't wait up for me.'

I went from the buffet to the ballroom and from the ballroom to the bar and got myself a drink. Anyone who may have arrived unpaired was by now paired and I was beginning to feel like a spectre at a feast. The sense of euphoria which the conversation with Pippa had given me was beginning to fade and I looked around for Sue in the hope that she might repeat the offer to take me to a party, but she was talking to a lean, balding figure in a beautifully cut suit, no doubt a hand-picked eligible. For a moment I even considered the possibility of asking my sister if I could tag along to her party, but thought better of it. In any case, knowing my sister, she would have probably said no.

I took another drink but instead of making me feel better, it made me feel worse. Holtzhacker had introduced me to drink early in life, but its effect was merely to enhance the mood I was in. When merry, it made me feel merrier, when depressed, it made me suicidal. The party, as far as I was concerned, was over.

When I got home father was sitting over the radio with a drawn face listening to the news in Polish.

CHAPTER THREE

Father had a theory that misfortunes hunted in packs. Everything one touched either turned to gold, or turned to ashes, and that, if his own experience was anything to go by, fate did not allow for anything in between.

He had been troubled by external events ever since the rise of Hitler, but he could at least comfort himself with the thought that things at home were going well. His business was prospering. I was doing well at school, and Sosh was not doing badly, but, perhaps more important, we, or at least Sosh, seemed to be on the brink of an ascent to a higher firmament.

The night of Pippa's ball possibly represented the high point in his fortunes. When I got back on my own he asked me what I had done with Sosh.

'She went on to a party.'

'What do you mean she went on to a party? You've just come from a party.'

'She went on to another party.'

'At this hour? It's nearly midnight. Who's looking after her?'

The idea that Sosh, even at sixteen, needed looking after, was laughable, but I told him that she was with Edwin.

'Edwin? Not Edwin Rodgers?'

'Yes, Edwin Rodgers.'

At which he went upstairs, no doubt to wake up mother to give her the glad news that her daughter was now moving in high society.

After that things began to go wrong.

Sosh was in some ways brighter than me, for while my academic success was due largely to persistent hard work, she seemed to get by without doing any work at all, and father, who liked to think that there was more to his daughter than a pretty face (and, if truth be told, a nasty temper) began to speak of her as a prospective doctor. She had expressed no such interest herself, but he could not imagine an outlet for academic skill other than medicine. He of course presumed, without ever raising the matter with me, that I too would be a doctor. Perhaps he hoped to open a clinic.

To expect a son to be a doctor was part of the syndrome of Jewish parenthood. To expect the same of a daughter – especially when she rarely opened a book – was asking a bit much of fortune. She had been able to get by in the lower school without effort, but about half-way through her fifth year my parents were summoned by her headmistress and told that it might be in the interests of both Sosh and the school, if she was removed.

It came completely out of the blue, and father's first reaction was predictable:

'The woman's an anti-semite.'

The odd thing about it all was that Sosh herself was surprised and upset, for if she was not inclined to work, neither was she inclined to leave school, if only because most of her friends were still at school, and she enjoyed the double life of schoolgirl on weekdays and temptress at weekends, and for the rest of that term she applied herself with sufficient diligence to earn a reprieve. As far as my parents were concerned, however, the damage was done.

Father would sometimes comfort himself with an old Yiddish proverb: 'If you've got *tzorus* from your children, no *naches* can comfort you, and if you've got *naches* from your children, no *tzorus* can hurt you', but having been dramatically robbed of his illusions about his daughter, he began to wonder if he was not deluding himself about his son.

And in a way he was, for although I was continuing to come away with the occasional school prize, I only had a real aptitude in maths and had no intention of studying anything else. I did not have the heart to tell him that, far from having two doctors in the family, he would have none.

It was about this rather fraught period that we had to go up to Glasgow to celebrate the Barmitzvah of Bernard, or Berale, Boyarski. Our second (or rather third) cousins had by then increased to four, and included a cross-eyed little girl with a spotty complexion, called Flora.

The father had trained himself to be a *mohel* (circumciser) and exacted a head-tax (if that's the word for it) on every second or third Jewish male born in Scotland, and they lived in a comfortable, well-furnished flat. Mrs Boyarski, now that her breeding days were over, had lost weight, acquired a new set of teeth, and looked almost stylish especially next to my mother. Bernard had won a scholarship to a local Grammar School (Allan Glen's), and although it was not Manchester Grammar School, he excelled both in English and maths and was a good athlete.

He not only read a portion from the Torah, as required of all Barmitzvah boys, but conducted the whole service, and the reception which followed was well attended by young and old, none of which surprised me. What did surprise me, was the presence of non-Jewish friends.

Although I had numerous non-Jewish acquaintances and was on fairly friendly terms with several non-Jewish boys at school, they never invited me back to their homes and I never invited them to mine. There was one boy called Stephen whom I had intended to invite to my Barmitzvah, but then I began to wonder what he would make of all the outlandish ceremonies and rituals, and changed my mind, yet here was a youngster with the snow hardly melted on his boots, who was on close enough terms with goyim to have them at his Barmitzvah.

Father had taken us to Glasgow as his good deed. 'We're the nearest thing they have to relatives in this country,' he said, 'so we've got to go.' He presumably thought there would be hardly anyone else there, and was a little taken aback to find the family prospering and at the centre of communal life. The one advantage of having poor relatives is that one can patronize them, but in Glasgow he almost found himself being patronized, and the rise of the Boyarskis, in a way, underlined his own decline.

I had more than a vague idea that things were beginning to go badly, but I found it difficult to discuss anything with father, for he did not converse so much as declaim, and if I wanted to know what was happening in his business I would ask mother. She herself, however, was in the dark.

'It's not that he won't tell me,' she explained, 'it's that his right hand doesn't know what his left is doing.'

I was in my final year at school, there was no certainty that I would win a scholarship to University, and I wondered if, in the circumstances, he would be in a position to pay for my fees.

'That you mustn't even discuss with him. If necessary he'll sell the business to pay for your fees.'

'He mightn't have a business to sell by then.'

'So he'll sell the house, but don't talk about not going to University.'

He used to cope well while his business was small and he could keep his accounts in a penny notebook and his files in a shoebox. When his business grew to the point where he had to keep ledgers and employ clerks and accountants and lawyers and insurance brokers, he got lost, and his whole operation ceased to make sense.

'The more I'm making, the more I'm losing,' he complained. 'When I had a small shop with broken windows and a leaking roof, and one old woman working for me, I was all right. Now I've got a whole warehouse with twelve people working for me, my accountants tell me I'm losing money. I curse the day I started having anything to do with accountants.'

He stopped eating, slept badly, lost weight. Mother became worried and insisted that he see a doctor.

'What for? He'll be like my accountant and tell me I'm dying.'

I suggested that he could economize by moving into a smaller house in a less expensive area of town, but there seemed to be an unwritten law that once one had moved into something better, it was unthinkable to move into something worse, for apart from anything else, it suggested a want of faith in one's Maker. It could also, as he pointed out, undermine the faith of one's creditors.

'To do well in business you've got to give the impression you're doing well. Once people think you're on the way down, they don't want to know you, and, what's worse, they don't want to know your children,' which I suspect may have been the crux of the matter, for he was afraid of anything which might check Sosh's advance into high society.

External events added to his private worries, but gradually they became part of them.

When I think back on the thirties, the one picture which consistently comes to mind is that of father bent over the radio, twiddling knobs, pressing buttons, and occasionally thumping the set for better reception, and one could hardly talk above the crackling noises and banshee squeals from distant stations.

He was, at first, not too troubled by the rise of Hitler, for he accepted the general wisdom that he was a passing phenomenon, and thought it might not be a bad thing if German Jews, or 'the Deutchers', as he called them, were shaken out of their complacency.

He came from a part of Poland which had once been under Prussian rule and there was no love lost between those Jews who had adapted themselves to German culture and thought of themselves as more German than the Kaiser, and those who like my father's family had remained obstinately Jewish.

'It takes a Hitler to keep some Jews Jewish,' he said, but as the Nazis tightened their grip on Germany, and began to threaten their neighbours, he revised his attitudes. The time for factional differences between Jews, and even for Jewish grievances against Poland, had passed. At first, whenever one spoke of Hitler, he would retort: 'He's no worse than the Poles.' Now he suddenly became a Polish patriot and let it be known that he had not only served in the Polish army under Pilsudski, but that he was in the cavalry.

Now though I could easily imagine father as a soldier, for he had a soldierly shape (before it was distended by gluttony and racked by bronchial ailments brought on by heavy smoking), I could not imagine him on a horse. With a horse and cart, certainly, but not on a horse, not on horseback.

And yet he had so many stories to tell of his exploits as a cavalryman, with all the attendant details, that I almost came to believe him.

'There we were, a platoon of us, ten troopers and an officer, Count Zamorski, a tiny man, almost a dwarf, on a huge black stallion, and ahead, covering the horizon, were the Bolsheviks, thousands of them. The sensible thing to do would have been to turn back, but you can't tell a Pole to turn back, not a cavalryman, not from the Bydgoscz Brigade, and certainly not a Zamorski. We drew sabres and cha-a-a-a-rged. We couldn't count the number of Bolsheviks we killed. The ground was littered with them like leaves in autumn.'

All of which did not stop him or mother worrying about relatives still in Poland. His own family was small, but mother had left behind elderly parents, brothers, sisters, uncles and aunts and countless cousins, nephews and nieces. She wrote to them all with offers of help and urging them to leave while they were still free to do so, and they wrote back reassuring letters that things in Poland were not as black as they seemed from England, that business was picking up and that, thank God, they were making a living.

I don't know what we would have done if her offers had been taken up, for father was by now hardly in a position to help anyone. As his business was largely with eastern Europe, he made desperate efforts to diversify, which may have been at the root of his trouble, for he branched out into areas in which he had few contacts and no experience, and in fact he seemed to spend most of his time by the radio. He had a smattering of half a dozen languages, including Russian, Polish, German, Ukrainian, Czech and – or so he claimed – Serbo-Croat, and he twiddled from station to station, from language to language, until he came upon a commentary or report which confirmed his darkest forebodings.

By the end of 1938 war seemed inevitable, and I decided that whether I won a scholarship or not, I would join the army. I had several grounds for my decision, among them, simple patriotism.

The very word patriotism sounds slightly archaic now and it has virtually become an obsolete emotion, but there was nothing obsolete about it in the thirties, certainly in our family. My father was a congenital patriot looking for a focus for his loyalties and became a British patriot long before he could speak English properly. When they played the national anthem in the cinema, he jumped to attention and, unlike everyone else, remained at attention till the last strains of the music had died away. In 1935 we all went to the pictures three times in one week, and sat through each performance twice, to see the newsreels of the Silver Jubilee Naval Review at

Spithead. He had been a Zionist, until two cousins who had been Zionist enough to actually settle in Palestine wrote that they had lost all their savings and were moving to South Africa. Even then he spoke vaguely of the possibility of settling in Palestine himself, but after the Naval Review, with all those battleships and cruisers and destroyers, and aircraft-carriers, and submarines, and frigates, stretched over the waters as far as the eye could see, he spoke of it no more, possibly because while he could envisage a Jewish state, he could not envisage a Jewish navy.

With me the matter was more complicated. There were many sets at the school, including a Bolshie set, and when the Spanish Civil War broke out, some of the older boys spoke of joining the International Brigade, and a few may even have done so. I shared their sympathies, if not their fervour. There was also a small Zionist set headed by a boy called Glauber who tried to convince me that Britain was on the brink of a Fascist coup and that there was no future for Jews outside their own homeland. Given the growing popularity of Mosley, and the triumph of Fascism in Spain, I did not find his argument unconvincing, but I was by now on the last lap of my studies and I was anxious to bring them to a successful conclusion, even if the world was to fall apart in the meanwhile. By the close of 1938, however, the press of events was such that even I was compelled to sit up and take notice, and I decided that if the country was to be at war again, I wanted to be out there in the front line.

My initial plan had been to go on to University to read maths and, if I took a good enough degree, to remain at University to teach maths, but now it seemed to me that a period of army service might be a welcome break from the cycle of sameness.

A little to my surprise Krieger reached exactly the same conclusion about the same time.

Once he entered upon his final year, even our Sunday excursions stopped and his application to work made me feel like a sluggard, and we saw nothing of each other outside school hours. When we decided to join the army, however, our friendship, which had become tenuous, deepened, and we began to enjoy the sort of camaraderie common among fighting men. The very thought of active service had a heartening effect on us both. Krieger, who had begun to droop, suddenly became erect, and even I felt I had grown an inch or two, until the black day when we both went to enlist and he was accepted, and I was not.

When the war broke out I went to University, my sister went into the Women's Land Army, and my father went bankrupt.

I had always thought that my father, whatever his failings, was a fairly astute business man, but his business might have failed without the benefit of war and a total ban on non-essential imports, but as his collapse coincided with the outbreak of hostilities, he could assume the martyred air of a war casualty instead of the abject look of a failure.

He had, in his more prosperous days, acquired a few properties which gave him a small income, and, by way of occupation, he listened to the radio both by day and night. He also took to going to synagogue more regularly, partly because it was a way of killing time, and partly because it was about the only place where he could hope to find an audience, and he gave hopeful commentaries on the progress of the war to all who cared to listen, and even to those who didn't.

Mother knitted for victory, and I dug. Most of our back garden had been taken up by an Anderson air-raid shelter, and I turned up what was left and planted vegetables.

My sister, for the time being, was the sole member of the family in uniform. She had never expressed an interest in agriculture but – no doubt influenced by the sort of company she kept – she had begun to show an interest in horses, which was why she joined the Women's Land Army. In her uniform of jodhpurs, green sweater, shortie coat and pork-pie hat, she seemed all set for a gymkhana, but she rarely caught sight of a horse and for the first year or so of her service, worked on allotments in a Manchester park, and lived at home.

The war had cut her off from her usual circle of admirers, but she quickly established a new one and a rapid succession of young, and not-so-young, men passed through the house. Father rarely spared them a glance, but one evening she came home in tow with a tall, debonair figure with three pips on each shoulder, at which father, busy as usual with the radio, sat up.

'You in the cavalry?' he asked.

'No, I'm in the Pay Corps, I'm afraid.'

At which father gave him a look which said, 'And for that they give you a uniform?' and returned to his twiddling.

Shortly after Dunkirk, father found, or was directed to, a job. It was, he let it be known, 'very secret' and he refused to say what he was doing, or even where he was doing it, and would answer every query with 'careless talk costs lives', or 'walls have ears', but it was perfectly obvious from other information he let slip that he was with Metropolitan Vickers at Trafford Park, and was presumably working on munitions. He had been issued with an army-type gas-mask in a canvas holder and when he slung it over his shoulder he looked and felt like half a soldier. He left early in the morning and returned late at night, exhausted but cheerful, with a weekly wage which surprised us all.

'We Jews think we're very clever,' he said. 'I'll tell you something, we're idiots. We like to be bosses, have our own business, be in charge, and so I had my own business, and what did it give me? Headaches, heartaches, *kadoches*. My life wasn't my own. Even when I came home in the evening and went on holiday, I was still in business worrying about money I owed, and worrying even more about money I was owed, about goods I ordered which didn't come, or goods which came but I didn't order, or faulty goods, or goods in store which didn't sell – and perishable goods at that. Sometimes when I was overstocked I nearly perished myself. So all right, I could dream of being a Rothschild, but at the end of it all I wasn't making much more, and sometimes I made a good bit less, than I'm earning now. And when I'm finished for the day, I'm finished for the day, and when I'm on holiday, I'm on holiday. I don't have to think about my work, or dream about it. I'm a free man. A businessman's a slave, and business is a jungle with everybody eating everybody else. In a factory you've got comradeship, friendship, mates, and you don't have to make a show of how much you're worth, or how much you'd like people to think you're worth, because everybody knows exactly what you earn. It's a *mechaye*. If I had known what it was to be a working man, I'd have become one the day I came here.'

His accent, which had been heavily Polish, became distinctly north country. He began drinking beer of an evening and ee-bah-gooming it over his pint, and, finally, to establish his solidarity with his newly found working-class mates, he bought himself a cloth cap and muffler. I was half-afraid he might begin to keep racing pigeons.

He was rather pleased with the figure he cut in his new attire and took to wearing it round the house; the first time my sister saw him she thought he was a tradesman who had come in to fix the plumbing. He virtually ceased going to synagogue and regarded those who did with disdain: 'These people don't know what it is to put in a good day's work,' he said. Presumably he found an audience for his war commentaries among his workmates.

For me, the first years of the war were fairly unhappy, not only because the news was depressing but because my personal circumstances were bleak, and there were times when they became almost desperate.

When I was rejected by the army, all sorts of wild ideas buzzed through my brain. I would join an ambulance unit! The fire service! The merchant navy! I would work in a munitions factory! But either because I was nervous of approaching any of them for fear of rejection, or because I am subject to recurrent bouts of common sense, I went to the one place which I was sure would have me, namely the University.

I didn't know what it was like in peace-time, but it was a cheerless place in war. The younger and abler dons had volunteered, or been conscripted, and various doddery old crocks had been brought out of retirement who generally preferred to reminisce about earlier wars than to lecture on mathematics. The abler, or at least the more robust members of my own generation had likewise been called up, and to be in University at all during those years was almost a confession of infirmity, and I wore no blazer, scarf, or tie which might have indicated my occupation (or lack of it). And yet I sometimes experienced odd moments of euphoria totally unrelated to my circumstances which I tended to distrust, for they were, not infrequently, preludes to disaster.

The first months of 1941 were cold, wet and blustery, with glowering clouds, as if the gods were angry with the world, but then one morning I woke to skies so clear and bright that I thought I was in another land. The trees, however, were still bare. The grass in the small park I crossed on the way to University, was still moth eaten, greyish and speckled with soot, and the ground was soggy underfoot, but it was sunny and warm, without a cloud in the sky, and towards evening the entire city was bathed in gold. I never thought Manchester could look so beautiful. The streets were clogged with military convoys, and the horizon was dotted with barrage-balloons, yet it was difficult to feel we were at war.

It was as if the earth had been given a brief golden hour before its final demise, for that night Manchester suffered its worst air-raid of the war and as the guns thundered and bombs crashed, I began to fear that nothing would be left of the place.

The sirens went about midnight. We had an air-raid shelter in the back garden, but it was festooned with spiders' webs, and as mother was more frightened of spiders than of bombs, we went downstairs to the kitchen, which was probably the least safe room in the house, but it *felt* safe. And there was the radio and the kettle so that we could comfort ourselves with successive cups of tea.

Our first anxiety was for father who was on night-shift at Trafford Park, which I presumed was the main target, but the fact that we were in some danger ourselves somehow diminished our anxieties.

The planes came in successive waves and we could hear the crump of distant explosions which grew louder as they came nearer, but the loudest noise of all came from a gun battery in a nearby park. The windows rattled. The floors quaked. The house shuddered and shook. Dust and soot came cascading down the chimney, sending up a black cloud which settled on everybody and everything. Then there came such an almighty crash that the whole house seemed to rise from its foundations, and I thought it must cave in, but somehow it remained intact, though paint came flaking from the ceiling like snow, and the air was heavy with the smell of broken masonry.

'Do you think he'll be all right?' said mother.

'He'll be all right.'

What else could I say? It seemed very unlikely that any of us would survive the night, yet I was hardly troubled by the thought, and it occurred to me that death possibly has no terrors where there is no prospect of survivors.

It was nearly dawn before the all-clear went.

Mother was asleep in her chair. I put a blanket over her, tucked it round her legs and tried to phone Trafford Park. The phone, as I anticipated, was out of order and I was surprised that we still had light, gas and water. I made myself a cup of tea, sipped it slowly, then went outside.

Much of Manchester seemed to be on fire with large flames leaping to the skies and smaller conflagrations flickering in every direction. It was mid-March, though it could have been midsummer, for warm breezes came wafting through the air. A thick pall of smoke hung over the city and hot ash descended from the skies in fine particles. Our own street was intact, but a nearby church had been gutted and its steeple had crashed to the ground.

Other people were emerging dazedly from their homes in ones or twos, to look around them and marvelling, as I did, not so much at the extent of the devastation, but that so much was intact. We talked in hushed voices, in awe, I suppose, at having survived at all.

I went back inside. Mother was trying to get through to Trafford Park.

'I've tried already. The line's dead.'

'Do you think he'll be all right?'

'Of course he will,' though now that we ourselves were out of danger I really was worried and kept reassuring her in an attempt to reassure myself.

I went to the police, but they could not tell me anything, and I went back to a breakfast which neither of us could eat. I did not attempt to get to University.

The morning was almost over before father finally appeared, his face and clothes covered in dust and grime. There was no public transport and he had walked the five miles from Trafford Park through streets heaped with débris.

'Half of Manchester is gone,' he said.

A little later Malka and Kate drew up in a taxi.

People like Malka did not take taxis without good cause, so that taxis, like telegrams, represented bad news. They had been blasted out of their beds, and their roof had collapsed, but miraculously, they themselves had remained unscathed.

But that was not the only miracle. The same bomb which had blasted my aunt out of her bed seemed to have blasted her out of her lethargy, for there was life in her eyes and a tone to her voice. She was a different woman, though not necessarily a better one, for whereas in the past she had never opened her mouth, she now – as if in redress for all those years of silence – would hardly shut it.

When Holtzhacker vanished, father felt that he had nothing to reproach himself with as far as Malka was concerned: he had done everything an older brother might be expected to do for a younger sister, perhaps more. He had provided her with a husband, who had provided her with a child, and even if the husband had proved fickle, she had been left with a roof over her head, and a pension (to say nothing of free burial rights whenever she should require them).

Mother felt otherwise and argued that as father had known Holtzhacker for many years, he should have had more than an inkling of what sort of husband and father (to say nothing of what sort of Rabbi), he was likely to be, and she took Malka and her daughter under her own wing as her personal protégées. We would have them in for meals at least once a week, and to stay for the duration of most festivals, and if we went on holiday – which in those days meant a week in Southport or St Anne's – they came with us.

If Malka was uncomplaining, her daughter Kate was not, and made her feelings known through every orifice, and my early memories of her were of tears and puddles and slippery floors and wet mattresses, as I felt tempted to remind her when she emerged from her moist and malodorous cocoon to become the femme fatale of her generation.

Kate was evacuated to Blackpool on the outbreak of war; Malka let her house and went with her, and we all sighed with relief. It's an ill wind that blows no good, but the North, at first, suffered very little from air-raids, and, like many other evacuees, they returned after about a year, only to have their roof fall about them.

Everybody in those days doubled up with everybody else, and as Sosh had by then been posted to north Wales, it would have been natural for Malka and her daughter to use her room, but she was home frequently, and even if she wasn't, her room with its perfumes and powders, and lipsticks, and her pictures of past and present boyfriends (including Edwin Rodgers), was considered to be a sort of holy of holies. Put another way, my presence counted for less than my sister's absence, and I had to move with my books and my papers and my gramophone and my records out of my bedroom and into the living room.

Malka was not happy with the arrangement. 'It's very small,' she sniffed, looking round my room, which it was. 'It's more like a pantry,' said Kate. Mother thereupon offered to move out of her room, but father said: 'You can move if you like, but I'm staying put,' so that was that.

I suppose it was my involuntary exile, rather than her incessant chatter, which converted the affection and sympathy I had for my aunt into something like hatred.

If I had been a medical student my needs would have enjoyed greater priority, but once I made known my determination to read maths, father lost all respect for me.

'His brains have gone to his head,' he said to mother in an anguished voice. 'What can we do?'

'Nothing,' she said, but if he had to tolerate a lunatic in the family, it did not mean he had to strive officiously to keep him comfortable, and my exile was a measure of his disdain.

My room had been more than my room; it was my sanctuary. Once the door was closed, I could leave the world, and the heated voice of my father, behind me. I had covered my walls with reproductions of Goyas and El Grecos, and I had a small gas-ring. Here I could make coffee; here I could listen to my collection of Beethoven symphonies. Above all, here I could work undisturbed.

Our living room was not quite our living room in that we rarely lived there. More importantly, we rarely lit a fire there, and it had the damp, unhappy smell of neglect. What was worse, it was just across the hall from the kitchen, which was where we in fact did most of our living, much of our quarrelling and all of our cooking, and I didn't know which I found more disturbing, the smell of cooking or the sound of acrimony occasioned by the growing hostility between my father and his sister. And, as if that was not bad enough, I had to suffer the intrusions of my cousin Kate, by now ten or eleven, who wanted to know what I was doing, why I was doing it, and why I couldn't find anything better to do. Also, did I have a girlfriend and if not, why not?

I began to dread mealtimes. Father was large, but with a compact, contained largeness, and mother was small, so that our kitchen had always seemed spacious. All that changed the moment Malka moved in, for with her broad shoulders, huge biceps, massive bosom and great arse, she filled up the place.

'The funny thing is the less I eat the more weight I put on,' she said. 'I wasn't like this before the war,' which was true, but if she ate little at meals, she never stopped nibbling between meals – now a piece of bread, now a cold potato, a carrot, a piece of cake – and if she wasn't chattering, she was grinding.

She was also presumptuous.

'I don't know why you waste your time, listening to all the news,' she said to father. 'It's not as if listening to the news will change the news, and it's always the same sort of news anyway. The wireless going all the time is getting on my nerves.'

At which mother suggested that he turn the radio down: he responded by turning it up.

'Nathan!' said mother.

'Leave him alone,' said Malka. 'He was like that as a child, selfish from the day he was born.'

'Nathan,' shouted mother, 'I can't hear myself talking.'

'And I can't hear myself listening,' and he switched off the radio and strode out of the room.

Then there was the matter of rations. Malka bought her rations of butter, sugar, eggs and whatever with her own money, which was fair enough, but she always took them up to her room last thing at night.

'You think we're going to steal them?' asked father.

'No, but that way we don't quarrel.'

'Nathan,' said mother, 'it's none of your business what Malka does with her rations.'

'It's not a question of my business. For all I care she can shove them up her fat – '

'Nathan!'

And added to the angry words, were the angry looks and the – albeit rare – angry silences, and I could no longer even escape to my own room.

Father and mother rarely went out together and when they did, mother usually insisted that they take Malka with them, which did nothing to enhance my father's affection for his sister.

One evening, all three were out to the pictures, Kate was upstairs in bed, and I was downstairs working, when a tousled red head appeared at the door, and a pair of mischievous blue eyes smiled at me. Looking at those eyes, I could see Holtzhacker.

'Why aren't you in bed?' I demanded in my best schoolmasterly voice.

'Can't sleep. Will you come up to my room and tell me a story?'

'No.'

'Will you tell me a story if I stay in here?'

'If I must.'

At which she climbed on my knee, digging her sharp knees into my groin as she did so, and put her arms round my neck.

'Are you comfortable?' I said.

'I'd be more comfortable in bed.'

'I am not coming up to your – ' But she cut me short.

'Look, there's something moving in your trousers – is it a mouse?'

I was too dumbfounded to answer.

'No, it's too big for a mouse, it must be a rat. Can I stroke it?'

At which I recovered both my voice and my sanity, grabbed her by the hand, rushed her up the stairs, pushed her into her room, slammed the door shut, staggered down the stairs, and collapsed into my chair.

I became afraid that unless she and her mother moved out very soon, we would have a child molester – to say nothing of a molested child – in the family (though it would be a moot point as to who was molesting whom).

There were also times when I feared bloodshed. Father was often on night-shift, and when he was resting, mother and I – and even Sosh, when at home – moved around like mice. Not so Malka, and one afternoon when she was in the kitchen with the radio on full blast, father came storming down the stairs in his long-johns and, if mother had not appeared at that moment, he would have gone for her with a meat-axe.

The next evening we had a family confabulation.

'They've been three months here now,' said father, 'which is long enough for anybody. Either they go, or I go.'

I concurred, and even mother sat there looking very unhappy, but did not disagree.

What, so to speak, brought a stay of execution, was Hitler's invasion of Russia.

When father first heard the news, he couldn't believe it and quickly twirled from station to station till it was confirmed in about six languages, after which everything else went out of his mind, and by the end of the week we nearly went out of ours. It so happened that he was home on sick leave for a week, and during the whole of that time there was hardly an hour of the day or night in which the radio was not going full blast. I cannot recall the nature of the ailment which kept him home, but he forgot about it himself. He also forgot his exploits under Pilsudski against the Bolsheviks, spoke of the tenacity and valour of the Russian soldier and I half-expected to hear that he was in the Red cavalry.

'Hitler's finished now,' he declared. 'Start with Russia and you finish with the devil. If it was too much for Napoleon, it will be too much for him. Napoleon got as far as Moscow, he'll get no further than Bialystok.'

Which was not quite the case, but, like some of the radio commentators he followed, he tried to make every Russian retreat seem like a tactical victory.

He took to buying Russian records and singing Russian songs and reading the *Daily Worker*, and mother, caught up in his enthusiasm, donated her silver fox to Mrs Churchill's Aid to Russia Fund.

Father did not actually join the Communist Party, but he began murmuring darkly about the coming revolution. 'When all this is over,' he said, 'it's not only Hitler who'll be finished, but the bosses.'

Yet at the same time he began sneaking back to synagogue, partly, no doubt, out of thanksgiving, but largely because the invasion of Russia called for the company of cognoscenti. Names like Bardia, Sidi Barani, Benghazi and Tobruk, were but distant places on an unfamiliar map, whereas Minsk, Pinsk and Vitebsk evoked personal histories, not all of them happy, but suddenly men who had exerted all their energies to establish themselves as Englishmen began to speak of themselves as Russians. Synagogues became operations rooms and many a congregant who came to pray stayed to explain what he would do if he were Timoshenko or Rokossovsky, and to consider Hitler's chances of crossing the Beresina or the Dnieper. Father, while on home ground, was thus one expert among many, but the fact that he was a comparatively recent immigrant gave him a greater authority.

I, in the meantime, was continuing to plod on half-heartedly through my University course.

University can seem an irrelevant place at the best of times, but it was now so removed from the tumultuous outside world that I went from lecture to lecture, and from examination hall to examination hall as if in a dream, and I established the habit of going to the pictures at least one afternoon a week almost in a bid to savour reality. It did not matter what I saw, for if I did not enjoy the main picture, or the second one, there was usually something worthwhile in the newsreel and failing all else there was always the cartoon. But what I saw on screen was almost immaterial. The cinema was a seedy building in a seedy part of town, but I found the darkness comforting, and even the musty, dusty smells, possibly because they reminded me of the synagogue I used to attend as a boy. I was only twenty and already pining for the old days when father was Life President, Holtzhacker was Rabbi, God was in his heaven, Malka was in her own home, and I was the golden boy of the congregation.

Sometimes, if I saw a really good picture, it could do more

for my spirits than a personal triumph. One afternoon I saw a particularly entertaining film with Deanna Durbin called *Spring Parade*. It was a cold, blustery autumn day, but I came away trailing a sense of spring and whistling a happy tune, when I saw a familiar figure in an unfamiliar guise coming towards me, and for a moment I was uncertain whether it was her in person or whether she had been conjured up by my mood. She certainly would not have been out of place on a cinema screen. It was Pippa in the uniform of an officer in the Women's Royal Naval Service (the 'Wrens').

'Do I salute?' I said, 'or do I pipe you on board?'

'You buy me a cup of tea,' she said, 'I'm freezing.'

We went to a nearby tea-room. The place was crowded and I felt extremely awkward. She had cut her hair short and she looked so neat, so trim and so beautiful, and I felt, and no doubt looked, so scruffy and unlovely that I could almost hear voices mutter: 'What's that doll doing with that tramp?'

I normally took considerable care with my dress and people used to remark on my dapper appearance, but apart from my attendance at lectures, I rarely went anywhere or saw anyone and I used the excuse of the war to let my natural slovenliness assert itself. Moreover, clothes-rationing had been introduced recently – Sosh had stolen half my coupons as well as those of my parents – so that it was almost patriotic to look shabby, but I had nevertheless overdone it. My trousers were baggy; my lapels curled; my cuffs frayed, and I hadn't shaved that morning.

'I'm sorry about my appearance,' I said. 'I wasn't expecting company, especially your company.'

'It's all right, I'm exactly the same the moment I get out of uniform. It's a reaction to all the regimentation,' which might have been a comforting thought, but for the fact that I had yet to be regimented, which led inevitably to a topic I would rather have avoided.

I couldn't tell her that I was rejected by the army and said that I had been deferred.

'You'll get a commission the moment you qualify,' she said.

'I wouldn't be so sure,' I said, trying hard not to sound too modest.

'You'll get a commission all right,' she insisted, 'unless you take active steps to avoid it. The army's growing so fast, they're scattering pips like confetti. Even Edwin, my brother – remember him? He's a lieutenant and within sight of being a captain.'

'Your father must be very proud of his progeny.'

'He's been very ill, poor chap, hardly knows what's happening. That's why I'm here. His memory hasn't gone, but it flickers on and off. Sometimes he has almost total recall and picks up things he's forgotten years ago. At other times he's almost a blank, but some people and things stay in the mind all the time, and you're one of them. He's always taken great pride in his ability to pick winners and takes an almost fatherly pride in your achievements.'

'Achievements? What achievements? I've done nothing about which even my father could boast since he last saw me.'

'He'd welcome a visit all the same. He can't get out much, and hardly sees anyone. Edwin's in Egypt and I'm in Devonport, and he and mummy are getting to an age when they can't do much with each other except quarrel.'

'Your father didn't strike me as a quarrelsome type.'

'He's not, but he's got a quarrelsome streak and mummy's just the type to bring it out. She's not too well either, as a matter of fact. They're both pretty sick, of each other mostly. They'd welcome a new face.'

I said I would try and drop in and it was only then that she added, almost as an afterthought, that they had sold their house and were now living in Buxton.

'It's quieter there and the air is better. Why don't you treat yourself to a day off? Buxton itself is lovely, and so is the scenery en route. You'll enjoy it.'

I said I would think about it but promptly forgot until, as fate would have it, my parents decided to spend a weekend in Buxton, and their decision brought on a crisis.

When father first broached the idea, mother said: 'But what about Malka?'

'What about her?'

'We can't leave her here on her own.'

'I want a break, I need a break – '

'She also needs a break.'

'In the neck she needs it.'

'You're forgetting what she's been through.'

'What she's been through? You're forgetting what I'm going through.'

'I'll tell you what,' said mother, 'why don't you go on your own?'

At which he threw up his arms and turned to me. 'I can't argue with her. You try.'

I had learnt how to cope with father's tyranny, but felt helpless in the face of mother's solicitude, especially as it was usually accompanied by steely determination, but this time my sympathies were entirely with father and I asked her if she didn't think he was right.

'Of course he's right,' she said. 'If he was wrong there'd be no problem, but I know Malka. She'll be upset.'

'And father isn't upset?'

'Of course he is, but he's also got blessings. She hasn't had anything but upsets, poor woman, and the child is so difficult.'

'No more difficult than the mother. She lived quite happily on her own before she was bombed out, you know.'

'She was in her own home then, she's our guest now.'

'Mother, no one can remain a guest for ever. Any reasonable person would have turfed her out months ago. We agreed she should leave last June. It's November now, and she's still here. She could be here for ever.'

'It's not easy to find a place.'

'She hasn't tried, and as long as you keep her snug she won't be trying, and why should she? You do all the cooking and most of the cleaning – '

'She does the shopping.'

'Only because she doesn't trust you with the rations. Look at yourself, you're worn out. Look at father. She's reducing you both to wrecks.'

'You're not looking so good yourself.'

'If I'm not, you know who to blame. You've got to go away, you and father, on your own.'

'How can I?'

'By packing your bags and taking a train,' I shouted.

It was the first time in my life that I had raised my voice to mother, but it worked. She went.

But before going she prepared food for the days she would be away and, not wishing to burden Malka unduly, she told me what would be in the oven, and what in the larder (we had no refrigerator in those days – few people did), and what to serve when. She must have debauched an entire week's rations on those two days, for they were substantial meals, but I nearly choked on them.

If Malka had uttered one word of complaint about being left behind, I would have exploded in her face. Kate did complain, several times. 'I've never been away ever,' she lamented, 'not since we came here,' but her mother said nothing. She sniffed frequently, however, wiped her nose and eyes, turned her food over, as a farmer turned hay, without eating much, and exuded a sort of chilly mist.

I suffered her silence and her sniffing, her sniffing and her silence, both at the Friday night meal and at the Saturday lunch. Mother (in spite of father's protests) had suggested that if the weather was fine, I could bring them both over on Sunday. The weather was fine, but I couldn't face another day in their company, and so I went on my own. Once I got there, though, I wasn't too sure how I would face mother and, on impulse, instead of going on straight to the hotel I went round to see Pippa's parents.

They lived in a run-down house in a run-down terrace which, at first, showed no signs of habitation. I rang the bell and knocked at the door for about five minutes, and was about to give up when a white-haired elderly figure in a dressing-gown came shuffling to the door and, as I anticipated, looked at me without recognition.

'I'm Sammy Hoch,' I said, 'Nathan's boy – Pippa's friend.'

I'm not sure if he knew who I was even then, but he led the way inside, slowly and falteringly. 'She's an officer, y'know,' he said over his shoulder, 'so is Edwin. Don't know what the army's coming to. That's the good thing about the war, though. Helps people like Edwin find his feet.'

He apologized for his own appearance and the state of the house. It was much bigger than it appeared from outside, and much messier and the air was heavy with the smells of decaying food, decaying furniture, decaying lives.

'Wife's away. Staying with friends in Harrogate. Impossible to get servants these days. Still, we all have to rough it one way or another these days, don't we? Drink?'

He poured some whisky into a dusty glass, and replenished a glass he had been drinking.

'Can't give you too much, I'm afraid. Not too easy to come by, this stuff. You in the army yourself?'

'Not yet.'

'You will be, no doubt. Did I tell you Edwin's an officer? Don't know what the army's coming to, still that's the good thing about the war. Helps people like Edwin. Not a patch on the first one though, is it? No trenches or anything like that. I was gassed in the first one. Saved my life. If you were shot or anything like that, they patched you up and sent you back for a second innings. Very few chaps came back from a second innings, not all that many came back from a first. You in the army yourself?'

'Not yet.'

And so it went on in ever decreasing circles, and I became bored and depressed. I could see why Pippa had been so insistent that I visit him. The poor man was senile and she was trying to enlarge his circle of visitors because he must have bored all his closer acquaintances out of their wits. Yet I was curious to know what had caused the transformation in his health and circumstances in the few years since I had seen him.

I told him I was studying maths, and – sounding curiously like father – he asked: 'Is there a livelihood in that?'

'It's too early to say.'

'Don't know what Edwin will do with himself when the war's over. Regular army, I suppose, but you need money for that. Can't live on a soldier's pay.'

I hated to be intrusive, but curiosity got the better of me. 'Forgive me,' I said, 'but haven't you got money?'

'Not a bean, dear boy. All gone.'

'May I ask what happened?'

'Not too sure myself. Been ill, you see. I'm much better now, but I was very poorly, and things began to fall apart. War didn't help.' He began to shiver. 'Has it turned cold, or am I imagining it?' For a day in late November it had, in fact, been uncommonly mild, but now that the sun was setting, it began to get cold, and I was feeling the chill myself.

'Central heating's conked out, can't get the spare parts. Would you be a good chap and pass me that travel rug over there?'

I got him the rug and put it over him.

'Have you no heating at all?'

'There's a radiator somewhere about the place, upstairs I think. One of the bedrooms. Sorry about the look of the place. Can't get domestic help, you see. Or at least you can, but they never stay. A drink?'

'No, thank you.'

'I think I'll have another, though goodness knows where the next bottle'll come from when this one's gone. Can't get the stuff for love nor money. Nothing much you can get these days, is there?'

I went upstairs and began my search amid a chaos of unmade beds, dirty linen, unwashed glasses, half-eaten sandwiches, sticky bottles and crumpled newspapers, and eventually found an electric radiator under one of the beds beside an unemptied chamber-pot.

When I came downstairs he was fast asleep, his head thrown back, his mouth open, snoring.

I looked at the broken, pitiful figure and couldn't help comparing him with the large, genial, self-assured aristocrat I had known only a few years before. I remembered how he had said then, 'the party's over', as if he had some premonition of what lay ahead.

I stood there wondering what to do next. I had come ostensibly to see my parents, and their hotel was only a few streets away, but I wasn't at all sure if he could be left on his own. On the other hand, what would have happened if I hadn't called?

A minute later the door opened and his wife appeared. She stared at me open-mouthed for a moment. 'Good God, what are you doing here?'

I told her about my meeting with Pippa.

'You've been seeing Pippa!' I didn't care for the note of surprise in her voice, laced as it was with disapproval, as if Pippa had no right to be consorting with the likes of me. Even amid the shambles in which we now stood, I still failed to qualify as a hand-picked eligible, but she recovered herself sufficiently to add: 'Very nice of you to come all this way. He doesn't have much company these days, poor man.'

It was only then that she seemed to become aware of the state of the house. 'What a bloody mess. Did you find him here on his own? Wasn't there a woman here?'

'No, no one.'

At which she sank into a chair and put her hands to her face. 'I don't know what to do. I had to go away for a couple of days, I just had to, I felt I was going mad. I paid a woman to look after him, clean the place up a bit, and make him something to eat. She must have walked out, the bitch.'

She then noticed a large envelope on the mantelpiece, and jumped up and tore it open. There was some money inside, and a note. After reading it and re-reading it, she passed it on to me. The handwriting was barely legible, but the message was unmistakable: 'I'm a respectable woman. You can keep your money. I've a good mind to go to the police.'

Her eyes filled up. 'I don't know what to do. It's happened before, but they were young girls – one was only a schoolgirl – so I was asking for trouble, but this was a matronly woman in her fifties, grey haired, a grandmother. I suppose he wants to reassure himself that he's not as old as he is, or as sick as he is. Look at him. You never knew him in his prime. This sorry heap was once a god of a man, tall, blond, dashing. Who would have believed he would end up like this? I sometimes feel tempted to put a pillow over his face to put him out of his misery.'

She sank back into her chair, tears pouring down her cheeks.

I stood there, helpless and desolate.

'Is there anything I can do?'.

She shook her head.

'Can't I make a cup of tea or something?'

'Tea? I doubt if there's a clean cup in the place.' And she wiped her eyes, jumped to her feet, threw off her coat, and put on an apron.

'Who'd have thought I'd have to skivvy at my age,' she said. I liked her in her apron, for it made her look purposeful and down to earth, though with her diamond earrings, pearl necklace and bracelets, she did not quite look the skivvy she imagined herself to be.

'I'll wash up,' I said.

She was touched by that and kissed me on the forehead.

'I'll wash up, but you can dry if you wish.'

When we finished with the crockery and cutlery and cleaned up the kitchen, she made tea and was quite cheerful by then.

'You're such a nice young man,' she said, 'pity we didn't see more of you. Alfred was particularly fond of you.'

'How could he be? We only met four or five times, and only on state occasions, Christmas dinners, coming-out balls – '

'I know, but you see he's always been disappointed in our children.'

'Disappointed in Pippa?'

'Pippa's not our only child, and even she is not quite the joy she looks. She has a pretty face but an awkward personality, and she's so unsure what to do with herself. She's all right now while the war's on – wars were made for the undecided – but God knows what she'll do when it's over. I used to think that with her face, and her figure and all that money, she would soon be married. And you can't imagine the number of eligible young men she's turned down, and from the best families, the best. I can't see her marrying now, not in the near future. Besides, the money's gone. Who knows how long she'll keep her looks?'

'If she keeps them for half as long as her mother she should be all right.'

She smiled at that and squeezed my knee affectionately. 'Seriously though, I'm worried about her. She's never able to finish anything she starts or to hold on to anyone she knows. I'm surprised she's lasted in the Wrens long enough to get a commission, and even then she was nearly cashiered for insubordination. She's a handful. As for Edwin, he seems to have found his feet at last, but that's all very recent, and I'm not sure if Alfred's taken it in.'

'Perhaps I caught him in a lucid moment, but we had a perfectly coherent conversation.'

'Didn't he keep repeating himself?'

'All the time, but he mentioned Edwin's commission with great pride.'

'I sometimes wonder if he saves one face for his visitors and another for me. In recent weeks he seemed to have lapsed into a dark despair. It's so unlike him. He had many attractive qualities – '

'If you'll forgive me, it's you who seems to be lapsing into despair. Listen to yourself, you're already talking in the past tense.'

'But it is all past. He was a large, genial man, with never a care in the world – it's the main reason I married him – but it all registered somewhere and accumulated with interest, though business difficulties didn't help.'

'When did it all happen?'

'Shortly before the war, and everything seemed to happen at once so that I'm no longer even certain whether the collapse in business brought on the collapse in health, or vice versa. He's made a marvellous recovery, all things considered. His memory went for a while, but it's come back in dribs and drabs. He often used to say, "Hasn't that young chap done marvellously?" – he could never remember your name I'm afraid – "Good to see I've done one thing right."'

'What did he mean?'

'Didn't your parents tell you how they came to be in Manchester?'

'I gather you helped them in some way.'

'About twenty years ago we got a letter from your father, right out of the blue. I hadn't seen him since I was a child, I hardly even remembered him, and I had no idea how he got hold of my address. It was long and rambling and full of sorrows about the hardships of life in Poland. He was married with two children and wanted to make a fresh start, for their sakes, he said, not for his, and he wasn't sure where to go – America, South America, South Africa, England perhaps. We were, as you know, only vaguely related, and I had no sentimental feelings about Poland at all, quite the contrary. I didn't care for living reminders of the old days, and I was tempted to write back and tell him to do what everybody else was doing and go to America, which, in fact, would have been fairly sound advice. Then Alfred read the letter and said,

"You can't do that, the poor chap's asking for a hand." Your father didn't actually need money to come here, but we helped set him up in business, and ever since Alfred's looked upon you as a sort of protégé.'

'Then why were we kept at arm's length?'

'Is that what your father told you?'

'That's what I always felt.'

'When you were small you would have had to come with your parents, and your father, if you'll forgive me, is a dreadful bore. When you grew older we often discussed the possibility of having you and your sister with us over the holidays, but Edwin was such a dunce, and Pippa so impossible, that we thought the better of it. No doubt your father told you that we were ashamed of you as poor relations, but the simple fact of the matter is that we were ashamed of our own children. So there you have it.'

We went back into the living room. Her husband was still asleep in the armchair, his mouth still open.

'He should really be in bed,' she said, 'but I don't suppose the beds are made.'

'They're not.'

'You've been upstairs? What were you doing in the bedrooms?'

'I was looking for the heater.'

'Good God, I hate to think what you must have found there. The place is not usually in this state.' She seemed distressed again.

'Can I help make the beds?'

'No, no, you've been helpful enough as it is. I wouldn't want to keep you.'

'I'm not in a hurry.'

'You've still to get back to Manchester, presumably. It took me the better part of a day to get back from Harrogate. The queues are a mile long.'

'I don't mind.'

'You're embarrassing me. There's nothing more squalid than unmade beds and unwashed linen.'

'But I've already been upstairs and I don't see what there is to be embarrassed about. You've got a large house, a very sick husband, and no help. I understand the situation.'

She sighed and led the way upstairs.

The bedroom was a picture of squalor, but I revelled in it, for in an odd way it made me feel accepted. It was like being made privy to an innermost family secret. The baring of linen, especially of dirty linen, is a baring of souls.

I helped to gather pyjamas, socks, underwear, pillowslips and sheets and rammed them into an overflowing laundry basket, and became increasingly aware of her presence every moment I was there. Neither of us spoke. Then, as we were on our knees folding a sheet under the mattress, our fingers touched. A tremor ran through me and I grasped her hand as if to steady myself. She made no attempt to withdraw it, but looked smilingly into my eyes.

'You're not quite the innocent you look, are you?'

'I never knew I looked innocent.'

'I can see now why you were so anxious to come upstairs. Couldn't you have held my hand in the kitchen? You didn't feel like it, did you? Some men don't function till they're surrounded by squalor.'

I kissed her hand.

'Better not.'

'Why not?'

'Think of my age, and think of yours.'

'What has age got to do with it? A woman is either desirable or she's not.' I slipped a hand under her skirt and rested my fingers on a suspender clip.

She stood up, pulled up her skirt, undid her suspenders and pulled off her stockings.

'I want to make sure that whatever else happens you don't tear my silk stockings. They're about the last pair I have.'

I was by now tearing my own clothes off, with buttons flying in all directions, and threw myself upon her.

'Not so rough and not so fast,' she whispered, and got up and locked the door. 'It's your first time, isn't it?'

'How can you tell?'

'By your impatience. Now relax and leave everything to me.'

I must have fallen asleep immediately after and woke shivering, and alone, in a darkened room.

I switched on the light, put on my glasses, dressed,

washed, made the bed and went downstairs. She was in her apron again, cleaning the sink, and looked as if she had been crying.

'I was going to wake you. You'll miss your last train back to Manchester.'

'That doesn't worry me.'

'It worries me.'

'Can't I help – ?'

'You've been helpful enough. I don't want to sound inhospitable, but you had better go.'

It wasn't what she said, or even how she said it, which troubled me so much as the fact that she didn't even glance in my direction. I felt like the Gorgon in the presence of Perseus.

I picked up my coat and moved uncertainly towards the door, not knowing what I had done wrong and hoping that she might at least see me out.

'Goodbye,' I said.

'Goodbye,' she said, but without looking up.

I managed to scramble aboard the last train as it was pulling out of the station. It was packed as nearly all trains were in those days, but people got off at stops along the line, and I eventually managed to find a seat, and I was making myself comfortable when I found myself looking into the astonished faces of my parents. I wanted to be alone with my thoughts and they were about the last people I wanted to see at that moment.

'Were you on the train all the time?' father asked.

I didn't want to go into details about my visit to the Rodgers and said that I had hoped to have supper with them at their hotel, but that they had already left.

'If I had known the trains were so bad I'd have told you not to bother,' said mother. 'We had to leave early or we would never have got on.'

'Queues a mile long,' said father.

'Is Malka all right?' said mother.

'It's the only thing she could talk about all weekend,' father put in.

'She's fine,' I said.

'She didn't complain?'

'Not a word.'

When we got home the place was deserted. Mother looked around her with distress, like a dam bereft of her young.

'They've probably gone to the pictures,' said father, but the very emptiness of the place gave me the feeling that their absence was more permanent. I went into my room. All their possessions were gone, and the camp-bed on which Kate had slept was folded up.

'I knew she would be upset,' said mother wringing her hands, 'that's why I didn't want to go away.'

'She'll be back,' said father. 'People like Malka only leave at the point of a bayonet.' Which, as we discovered an hour later, was more or less what happened.

We did not have a bayonet in the house, but we had something approximating to it in the person of my sister. She had arrived unexpectedly to find Kate in her room putting on her lipstick and nail-varnish and drenched in her perfume. But that was perhaps the least of it. She had felt crumpled and grimy from her train journey and was desperate to have a bath, and Malka who was herself having a bath when she arrived had used up every drop of water in the house.

'I couldn't even wash my hands properly,' said Sosh.

'What happened then?' asked mother.

'I gave her a piece of my mind.'

'Good for you,' said father.

'But what did you actually say to her?'

She could not repeat her words in the presence of mother, but what she had actually said to her was: 'You great stupid cow. Does it never occur to you that there are other people in this house who might want a drop of water?' Upon which Malka went up to her room, packed, ordered a taxi, took her daughter by the hand, and left.

I could have kissed my sister. I immediately moved my possessions back to my room and, as far as I was concerned, the darkest days of the war were over.

CHAPTER FOUR

When America came into the war a week or so later, father picked mother up, swung her round the room and kissed her on the forehead.

'Can't you see what this means? It's over, finished. They're done for. Who can beat America, the richest and most powerful country in the world – and with six million Jews! All right, she can lose a few ships, but what's a battleship to America, or even an aircraft carrier?'

And when I eyed him without response he turned to mother and asked if there was anything wrong with me. Perhaps there was, but it could equally have been something right.

I was filled with a sweet sickness which left little room for external events, no matter how important or dramatic. If the world had come to an end, it would hardly have impinged upon my awareness. I was disinclined to eat, to talk, or even to work. Could I, I kept asking myself, be in love with a woman older than my mother? Or was it all merely the lingering aftermath of defloration?

I woke in the morning with the vision of Theresa before me, and fell asleep still hugging that same vision, and especially the moment she raised her skirt to remove her stockings. Yet the sweetness was mingled with confusion. Why had she turned so cold and hostile? Had I abused her hospitality, or was it simply a feeling of contrition?

I drafted letter after letter, each draft longer than the previous one, and finally tore them all up and sent her one line:

'Do you think I could possibly see you, if only to talk to you?'

She replied:

'Be sensible. I'm a married woman of fifty-five with a very

sick husband. No doubt we shall be bumping into each other again, but there is no point in writing to me or trying to see me, and you would do best to forget me.'

I, of course, couldn't forget her, and had no intention of doing so, but I was able, by throwing myself into my work, to ease her gradually out of my mind, which was just as well, for I was within sight of my exam finals.

I had not, in the previous few terms, applied myself to my work with my usual energy, partly because I was denied access to my room, and I told myself that it would not be the end of the world if, instead of obtaining the first class honours I hoped for, I ended up with a second, for there were people on every side of me who seemed capable of leading, happy, wholesome, and even successful, lives without the benefit of a degree at all. I was too obsessed with prizes and awards, I told myself, but after that letter I felt that I had to have a first, if only by way of consolation, and I buried myself in my room, emerging only for quick forays to the University library or to snatch a bite of food. I ceased to attend lectures because almost everything the lecturers had to say was available in their books. I doubt if I slept more than three hours in any one night, and when I did sleep, I often devised theorems in my dreams.

When I finally emerged from my hibernation, I found that Manchester was overrun with Americans, not a few of whom had laid siege to our house.

Sosh was still nominally in the Women's Land Army, and still stationed in Wales, but she seemed to be home every second day, and whenever she appeared, the Americans descended in force.

They came in all shapes and sizes, some in uniform, some in mufti, fat, thin, tall, short, some with stripes to their sleeves, some with bars to their shoulders, several with medals; soldiers, sailors, marines.

One evening, early in the war, Sosh had made the mistake of coming home with Edwin in tow and although he was, at the time, only a private, he was nevertheless a Rodgers, and father began to think of him as a prospective son-in-law, even though Sosh gave no hint that there was anything serious in their relationship, and even after he had been posted abroad, father was not particularly welcoming to anyone else she brought home. He was, however, prepared to make an exception of Americans, and treated officers with warmth, NCOs with tolerance, and privates with cold reserve, bordering, sometimes, upon open hostility. In the British army one could tell officers apart from other ranks even in mufti – indeed, especially in mufti – for they looked different, sounded differently, had different sorts of names, and even smelt differently.

In the American army, officers tended to be leaner than privates, and much leaner than NCOs, but otherwise they looked the same, sounded the same, smelt the same, and they were all Jays and Rays, Als and Hals, Murrays and Garys. Mother, for her part, treated them all alike, and they would arrive at all times of the day, and most hours of the night, so heavily laden with confections that father was tempted to open a sweet shop.

For all my sister's attractions, and even the goodwill engendered by mother, I was surprised they continued to come, for apart from the deterrent of father's hostility, there was the greater deterrent of his conversation. He had by now acquired a smoking-jacket (which mother had knitted for him) and a pipe, presumably because he thought it gave him greater authority. I suspect he modelled himself on J. B. Priestley, a broadcaster he much admired, who was also a pipe-smoker, and he adopted Priestley's ruminative tone and even something of his Yorkshire accent.

Father was not a mere chatter-box and, when caught among friends, he could be silent for minutes at a time, but strangers seemed to bring out the oracle in him and, wherever two or three foregathered, he felt compelled – with pipe in hand – to give his opinion on the events of the day. The Americans were a captive audience, and, as they were unfailingly polite, never interrupted, and listened with something like interest, he might have continued for ever, but for the intervention of mother.

I was curious to see upon whom Sosh's favours would finally alight, and there emerged from the mass a tall, lean, gangling youngster with a pointed chin, short nose, deep-set blue eyes and cropped, blond hair. His actual name was

Matthew, but everyone called him Sunny, and sunny he was in appearance and temperament. I was never too sure how Sosh felt about him (I was never too sure how she felt about anything), but father fell in love with him at first sight, and his face lit up every time he appeared.

'Is he Jewish?' he kept murmuring anxiously. 'He doesn't look it, and he doesn't behave it.'

I wasn't too sure what constituted Jewish behaviour or even Jewish looks, and said, 'Why don't you ask him or Sosh, for that matter.'

'You know what she's like,' said father, and in the event Sunny volunteered the information himself.

'If my head should be blown off, I'd be buried by a Jewish chaplain,' he said, which seemed to satisfy father. More, he was in heaven, for it turned out that he was also a qualified lawyer. He was not a Rodgers, but otherwise he had everything one could reasonably expect of a prospective son-in-law. He was American, an officer, a lawyer, Jewish and *didn't even look it*, which, paradoxically enough (for father regarded himself as a Jewish patriot), was a supreme quality.

He was also as courteous as only an American can be. He called father, Sir; mother, Ma'am; Sosh, Soshana, though he didn't seem to be quite sure what to make of me. When we invited him to join us for dinner one Friday night, he brought flowers for mother, cigars for father, perfume for Sosh, and a yard-long bar of Hershey's for me, which made me suspect that he thought I was a schoolboy.

It so happened that my examination results had come through about then. I received a first and, rather unexpectedly (though there wasn't much competition that year), I won a prize worth £100 in cash, and father opened the conversation with:

'Did Sosh tell you he got first place in Manchester University?' and when I hurried to correct him, he said: 'So, it still comes to the same thing.'

'Congratulations,' said Sunny. 'I suppose you'll be going into the army now.' At which there was an embarrassed silence, till father chirped in with: 'I was in the Polish cavalry myself...'

The young man sat through the monologue which followed, not only without a yawn, but with a semblance of rapt attention. It was all above and beyond the call of duty. I looked at mother several times in the hope that she might bring it to an end, but she must have felt it inappropriate to do so on such an occasion. I also glanced nervously at Sosh, for she did not suffer boredom lightly and could tell father to shut up whatever the occasion, but all her attention was focused on the young man, and I almost had the feeling that she was using the exposure to father as a test of his devotion. True love could have had no finer proof.

Mother must have taken father aside after the meal for a quiet word, or perhaps Sosh took him aside for a noisy one, for at subsequent encounters Sunny was allowed to open his mouth, and he told us that his parents were both lawyers, that he had a younger brother at college who was studying law, and two others who were still at school.

'Will they also be lawyers?' I asked.

'Could be,' he said, quite oblivious to the irony in my voice. 'Dad's quite a guy, and I suppose he's the model for us all.'

He began passing round photos, first of a tall, distinguished, grey-haired figure who not only looked successful, but whose expression said: 'See how successful I look.' Another showed a tiny, handsome, well-groomed woman, his mother. A third showed the whole family in a garden setting, with two labradors and a black maid.

'Is she also a lawyer?' I asked.

Sosh gave me a dark look, but he laughed: 'By contagion, you mean?'

He was, in some ways, too good to be true, amiable, good humoured, well mannered, well spoken, well read. His ears were slightly pointed and he reminded me a little of an overgrown gnome. He looked, and sounded, an innocent, especially next to Sosh, and I couldn't quite make out the basis of their relationship.

'You don't like him do you?' she said to me.

'Not like Sunny? What is there about him to dislike?'

'There isn't, that's why you don't like him, or at least you're jealous of him.'

There she was on firmer ground, for he was tall, a soldier,

an officer, while I was none of these things. I had thought of applying for a job in the civil service where my mathematical qualifications might be of some use, but my Professor had encouraged me to go in for a post-graduate degree at Cambridge and I was still waiting to be interviewed.

Then one morning, quite unexpectedly, I received my calling-up papers. I attached no particular importance to them for I had to undergo another medical and presumed I would fail the next one as I had failed the first one, but my doctor, who had served in the first war, told me: 'They'll take you all right, as long as you have enough breath to moisten a mirror.' He was right.

My acceptance for military service, in some ways, meant more to me than my first in maths, for almost everyone I knew was engaged in some form of war service and I was begining to feel like a cripple, so that the very thought of being in uniform was exciting.

Father was pleased with the news. 'You'll be an officer for sure, a captain, even a major, maybe,' and so confident was he of my rank that he thought it equipped me to handle a delicate domestic problem. Sosh and Sunny had been going out together now for about two months, and were seeing each other two or three times a week. 'I know he's serious about her,' he said, 'but is she serious about him?'

'Why don't you ask Sosh?' I said.

'You know what she's like. You're her big brother, she respects you.'

It was a long time since Sosh had last called me Titch or the Midget, but I was not at all sure whether she respected me or anyone else, and as a family we were rather poor at communicating with each other.

I had never had much difficulty in talking to mother about almost any subject, but even then I felt constraints, for she was parsimonious with time and never regarded conversation as an activity in its own right, but as something one did while doing something else, so that when we talked at all, she was knitting, or sewing or darning, and our eyes rarely met.

Father sometimes talked while he was eating, not infrequently with his mouth full, but otherwise when he engaged in conversation he applied himself wholeheartedly to it, but he rarely conversed with me, partly because – ever since I won that scholarship – he was slightly in awe of me. Whatever the cause, there was always some slight distance between us which grew wider as I grew older, and even when we did talk, we both tended to avoid anything personal.

If he was in awe of me, he was afraid (as we all were) of Sosh, for his little girl had a big mouth, though she did not, in fact, have to use it, for if provoked, or even if unprovoked, she could petrify him with a glance. In the main, however, she only snapped at him, not out of anger or exasperation or impatience, but because that was her normal way of talking when she was at home.

She modified her tone when addressing mother, but she nearly always snapped at me, which didn't worry me in the least, but it did have a limiting effect on conversation and if we exchanged as much as a sentence in the course of a day, it was a lot, and I was thus not too keen to fall in with father's wishes. Yet, now that I was about to go off to the wars, I felt obliged to establish some sort of rapport with her, and I invited her out to dinner.

At first she thought that she hadn't heard right. 'You're inviting me?'

'Yes.'

'To dinner?'

'Yes.'

'Where?'

'Anywhere you like.'

'The Midland?'

I faltered at that, but said: 'Yes, why not?'

'Golly, have you robbed a bank?'

'No, but I've won a hundred pounds which I haven't touched. There's nothing much you can spend money on these days.'

'Why don't you find yourself a pretty young girl to take out?'

'I don't know any pretty young girls – nor pretty old ones, for that matter, and in any case I want to have a word with you.'

She grinned at me for a moment with a half-amused expression, then said: 'All right, I will.'

We did it in style and went by taxi and I realized for the first time what a pretty sister I had.

I could hardly help being aware that she was attractive, but unbelievable as it may seem, I had never in the twenty or so years she had been about, taken a really close look at her face. As a family we rarely ate together except on Friday nights and Saturday lunch, and even then Sosh usually found some excuse to be away, but now, sitting across from her at a small round table I was able to scrutinize her in some detail. It had been a hot summer and the open-air life obviously suited her. She was deeply tanned, which brought out the brightness in her smile, and her face still had the slightly rounded quality of a child. She had good, regular teeth, freckles, green eyes flecked with gold, and black wavy hair, and when she smiled, little cavities formed on her cheeks and chin and even on the tip of her upturned nose. That nose, I felt, though pretty, was slightly too small, for though she was well proportioned, there was quite a lot of her. She often complained she was too big, but her size was so much a part of her personality, that I could not imagine her small.

I had intended, after I had had a drink or two, to ask about her plans, but instead she spent much of the evening questioning me about mine.

'Did you know I was worried about all that time you used to spend with Holtzhacker? I had thought of mentioning it to mother, but she wouldn't have known what I was talking about.'

'I'm not sure I know what you're talking about. Are you suggesting that I'm a pansy, or that Holtzhacker was?'

'The fact is I can't remember seeing you out with a girl, and as for Holtzhacker, I thought that Malka was a man – until she had Kate. I just didn't like the way he kept putting his hand on yours and the fond way he looked at you.'

'He was my uncle.'

'He was also my uncle, but if he had tried it on me I'd have socked him in the eye.'

'Men can be fond of men without being pansies, you know. Look at father and Sunny – do you think they're pansies?'

'I sometimes wonder.'

'You mustn't put sinister constructions upon perfectly normal and perfectly wholesome sentiments. I was very fond of Holtzhacker, he was good company.'

'For a young boy?'

'I was precocious in a way and I suppose I found boys of my own age too childish.'

'What about girls of your own age?'

I hesitated before answering. 'I suppose I also prefer the company of older women.'

'Who, for example?'

'I don't have to say,' and despite persistent questions as to why I didn't I managed, eventually, to lead the conversation back to Sunny.

'You don't like him do you?' she said.

'So you keep telling me. First of all, I do. Secondly, it wouldn't matter if I didn't, and thirdly, I've no idea why you should think I don't.'

'I can see it by the way you talk to him, and the way you look at him, and I can feel it when you're together. You resent him.'

'Why should I?'

'He's twice your height for a start.'

'We're back to that, are we? I assure you I have learned to live with the fact that I'm a dwarf.'

'You're not a dwarf, far from it, but he's very tall and very good-looking – I'm not saying that you're not good-looking, because you're rather handsome, in your compact way – '

'In my compact way!'

'I don't mean it as an insult.'

'I know, I know, you mean it as a compliment.'

'You'd be very attractive indeed, if you took off those awful glasses, but he's *very* good-looking – like a film star, and – ' She hesitated.

'And what?'

'I don't know how to put this, but you obviously think I'm in love with him.'

'What are you trying to say?'

'Well, you could be jealous.'

Upon which it all suddenly sank in.

'Good God, what conceit! Do you think that just because

half the American army is in love with you, I must fall for you as well? What sort of books have you been reading?'

'I once shared a billet with a girl who left home because her brother kept groping her, and rubbing himself against her whenever they were alone together, and he once tried to rape her.'

'Sosh, you're mad.'

'All right, if you don't want to talk frankly, change the subject.'

'I'm just amazed that such lunacies can get into your head. I assure you, beautiful as you are, I have never entertained any incestuous thoughts about you.'

'Haven't you? Well, you can't be normal, because I've often entertained incestuous thoughts about you. Remember the time I walked into the bathroom while you were in the bath.'

'How old was I, four?'

'Fourteen or fifteen, and I just stood there and stared – I could imagine what you'd been doing with yourself in the water, you dirty dog. You'll be telling me you don't remember. It made me feel deliciously moist. I daren't think what I'd have done if mother hadn't been shuffling around upstairs. All brothers and sisters have incestuous thoughts about one another, only not all act on them.'

'You've been spending too much time among farmyard animals, my girl. Let's change the subject.'

'If you insist.'

We ate silently for a time before I could proceed; I hardly felt like eating at all.

'I can be a monster, can't I?' she said.

'You can, but that's only because we've let you become one, and it's too late to do anything about it I suppose. Now can we get back to Sunny?'

'What about him?'

'Are you going to make an honest man of him?'

'Did father put you up to this?'

'What if he did? Don't you think he has a right to know?'

'I'm very fond of Sunny, but then who wouldn't be?'

'And I gather he has more than a passing fondness for you.'

'That's the trouble, he's crazy about me. He wasn't supposed to talk about it – they're not supposed to talk about anything – but it looks as if they'll all be sent abroad shortly, and he's threatened to desert rather than leave me. There's a soldier for you.'

'What did you say?'

'I told him to grow up. He's so immature. I suppose all men are, specially Americans. I thought Edwin was bad enough, but then he was hardly more than a schoolboy. Sunny's twenty-five. Father's not all that mature, if it comes to that. I've only been going out with Sunny these last six weeks, and he could be sent to the ends of the earth any day, so what's the point of pressing me about my feelings? Bloody hell, I'm only twenty. What's the hurry?'

'Look Sosh, nobody's in a hurry and nobody's pressing you, but we've grown up without being able to talk to each other. Father, as you know, is besotted with Sunny, and he would like to know what your feelings are and what your plans are.'

'Why doesn't he marry him himself?'

'He probably would if he could. Why don't you take him out one evening and talk to him as I'm talking to you now.'

'He's such a bloody fool, I've no time for him. I don't know how mother's been able to stand him all these years.'

'So what do I tell him?'

'You don't have to tell him anything. He shouldn't expect people to make serious decisions when everything's so unsettled and the unexpected keeps happening all the time.'

I called the waiter and paid the bill, and as we rose from the table two army officers entered the restaurant. One I hadn't seen before, the other was distinctly familiar. Familiar or not, he looked at me without recognition, but his eyes lit up at the sight of Sosh, and he took both her hands in his.

'My dear,' he said, 'it can't be you.'

It was Sefir Safran.

CHAPTER FIVE

Sergeant Major Pike regarded himself as something of a comedian and put on his usual Sergeant Major's act as he surveyed the line. His jaw sagged, his eyes bulged, he seemed to struggle for words, and when they finally came, they emerged as an awed (if amplified) whisper: 'God Christ Almighty! Where did they find you, under a fucking stone? It breaks my heart to look at you, it does.' His voice broke, and he looked as if he was going to cry. It was a convincing performance, and I suspect he meant it.

By the end of 1942 Britain was scraping the bottom of the barrel and it was obvious to even my untrained eye that we were not an élite but an oddly mixed bunch scooped up by fate, some on the edge of middle-age, some not yet out of boyhood, not a few on the point of collapse, and nearly all of a quality to put heart into a despondent enemy. At school and at University I had been among the crème-de-la-crème, here I was among the dross-de-la-dross, but I didn't mind it a bit. It was a relief to be in the army at all.

All my life, in so far as I moved at all, I had moved among Jews and book-worms, and it was mildly exciting to be among people who were neither one nor the other. I was also something of a loner, yet with a craving for company, and here one had company most times of the day, and all times of the night. The uniform alone proclaimed that I belonged, and helmeted, and with rifle and pack, I felt equipped for unimaginable acts of valour. The hob-nailed boots added a good inch to my height, and every time I jumped to attention – an action which sent a shudder from my heels to my head – I felt as if I had grown by another inch.

I was never quite the dwarf my sister made me out to be, but I was on the short side, and in my first years at school, when I was mercilessly bullied by the bigger boys, I yearned for the day when I would be big enough to bully others, but I never acquired the necessary size (or the necessary disposition) to do so, and I became self-conscious about my height, or lack of it, especially as nearly everyone around me was, if anything, overgrown. Towards the end of 1942, however, there must have been a round-up of everyone under 5′ 3″, for there were several men in my unit shorter than me, and one, called the Runt, who was so diminutive as to make me feel tall.

The centre of the base was a vast, prison-like E-shaped building looking out on a huge square, but most of us were housed in Nissen huts built in the surrounding meadows, and I was in a hut which, for reasons not difficult to imagine, was known as Farter's Castle.

We were all, given the nature of our diet, prone to quiet reports which, after a prolonged drinking session, could amount to a sustained barrage, but there were two men in our hut who farted as naturally and as frequently as they breathed. One was a Yorkshire mill-hand called Bilcombe who played in a brass band and could do better with his anus than his trombone. The other, called Hewitt, was an anal ventriloquist, a singular instance of *ars gratia artis*. He was a Catholic and during Mass would often let go when the Padre bent down to perform a holy office. He did the same for a Duchess in a velvet cloak who came down to lay the foundation stone of a new building, and for a visiting Cabinet Minister as he sat down to lunch in the officers' mess.

I can remember all the occupants of the hut, their names, their faces, their histories, where they slept, even how they smelt. I was seven years at Manchester Grammar and, with but few exceptions, my contemporaries remain a vague blur. Yet I was only three months in that hut and everything associated with it remains clear as if it happened yesterday.

It is said that there are no friendships like the friendship forged in war, but we were not quite at war and the greatest hazard we had to face during those months was the possibility of being shot in error (or perhaps not in error) by a fellow conscript. We did, however, have to face common hardships, and a common enemy in the person of Company Sergeant

Major Pike, though, for my part, I was at first inclined to regard Pike with respect, perhaps even affection.

During my first march in full kit, with him bellowing at my ear, I might have turned my rifle on him, and on myself, if it had been loaded, but when I survived the day and lived to march again I began to think there was something to be said for a little judicious bullying. I was emerging lighter and fitter in body and with energies I never knew I possessed.

I had never thought I was unhappy at home and was therefore surprised to find how much happier I was in the army, partly I suppose, because in spite of the petty harassments incidental to army life, it was a less pressurized existence. I may never have talked much to my family, but I was always aware of their anxieties, and it was a relief to be a stranger among strangers, and although we soon became intimates, we were never weighed down with mutual concern. One also acquired a passing sense of resignation. There was no need to scheme or plan, or give much thought for tomorrow. Everything ahead was set out by those on high and one only had to fall in with orders. Which does not, however, mean that it was a carefree existence.

I had never given much thought to the Jewish dietary laws in Manchester because I rarely ate out and mother kept a strictly kosher home, and I gave no thought to them in the army because there was a war on, and even if there hadn't been I preferred to fall in with the ways of the others, but there was in the hut a tall thin youngster, with long eyelashes and a face like a fawn, called Leibgot, who did keep kosher. He did not ask for a special diet, and I doubt if he would have got one if he had, but he hardly touched anything at table and sustained himself mainly with parcels from home, and the fact that he continued to keep kosher gave me slight qualms of conscience about the fact that I did not.

That, however, was not the only source of unease. Leibgot was the most awkward person I had come across. If there was a wrong way of doing a thing, he would do it, and even if there wasn't, he would try to find it. If we jumped to attention, he would stand at ease. If we wheeled left, he would wheel right, and if we could hear the clatter of a rifle falling on parade, we could be sure it was his. He could just about dismantle a rifle and put it together again, but when he tried to assemble a Bren gun he somehow managed to fix the barrel at right angles to the butt, and when it came to grenade drill we all dived for cover.

It all sounded so simple.

'You grip the grenade firmly in your right hand,' which he did. 'Remove the pin with the left,' which he did. 'Count five,' which he did. 'And throw,' at which he looked slightly confused.

'I said throw,' shrieked the sergeant.

'But in which direction?'

As the only other Jew in the hut, I was embarrassed, for his ineptitude was a reflection on the soldierly qualities of my race. I did my best to guide him and he certainly tried hard enough. Whenever we had a free afternoon and made for the nearest town, he would remain in barracks, polishing his boots, oiling his rifle, arranging his kit, studying his manuals, but to no avail. The harder he tried, the more awkward he became.

'I'll make a soldier of you yet, you fucking little lily,' growled CSM Pike, and what began as the usual parade-ground harassment gradually assumed the nature of a crucifixion, and in sunshine or rain one could see Leibgot, his rifle held high above his head, belting round the square at the double, with Pike bellowing after him.

'It's ablutions for you, m'lad, for the rest of your natural,' he told him, 'and you'll do me and yourself a favour if you stick your fucking head in the shit-hole and keep it there.'

There was in the hut a thick-set man with glasses and an old-Bill moustache whom we called Dad, for he was in his late thirties, who found the sight of the torments difficult to take and kept saying: 'That Pike wants a bayonet up his arse.' I took the trouble to go through King's Regulations and found Pike in breach on several counts, but, as I said, I had a sneaking respect for the man. I admired qualities I thought I lacked, and toughness was one of them, and I'm not sure if I did not despise the supine element in Leibgot. He never complained, though I sometimes thought I heard him sobbing quietly in the night, and Dad, obviously feeling that as a Jew I was under some obligation to look after my co-religionist, said to me: 'Why don't you go to the CO? He's got no right to treat him like that,' which he hadn't, but again, I was wary of playing the barrack-room lawyer, and I was sufficiently imbued with the public-school ethos to feel that going to the CO was a little like going to the beak. It was not the done thing.

There was a boy in the hut, a tall, languorous figure called Clayton who had been to a minor public school, and while we were training with explosives, in which he became quite expert, he seriously suggested arranging an accident and blowing Pike up, which perhaps shows how the public-school ethos works. Murder is all right, but telling tales is not, but then an incident occurred which left us with no option.

We were on a route-march in the rain one day, when Leibgot, with full pack, slipped and fell face first into a puddle, and Pike, who was right beside him, instead of going to his help, put a hob-nailed boot on his head and ground his face in the mud. The incident could not have lasted more than a few seconds, but in the course of those seconds Leibgot nearly died.

Four of us saw what happened and, without a word passing between us, two stopped to help Leibgot, while a further two went to report the incident to an officer at the rear of the column. He immediatelly pulled the column to a halt and went to investigate. A little later a tender pulled up and Leibgot, his face scratched and bleeding, accompanied by two medical orderlies, was driven back to camp. We were not too sure what happened to Pike, for we did not see him the rest of that day, but that night he came to our hut. We had just been to see Leibgot in sick-bay and there was a babble of excited voices which died away when he appeared.

'Let's lynch the bugger,' said the Runt. The rest of us remained silent.

'I know what you're feeling,' said Pike. 'I'd feel the same m'self, but there are one or two things you should know.' He pointed to the ribbons on his chest.

'See these? You don't get them for taking salt with your porridge, you know. This is the Military Medal, this is for being mentioned in dispatches, and so is this. This is the Mons Star. This I picked up in India, this in Iraq. Guess how long I've been in the fucking army? Go on, guess. Twenty-four fucking years, that's how long, and I faked my age to get in.'

He tore open his shirt and pulled up his vest.

'See these?' he said pointing to several ugly scars. 'They're not beauty spots, you know. Fucking shrapnel. A shell landed two yards away. Killed everyone in the platoon. They thought I was done for too, until I crawled back into the trench. That was in the first war, but the first one was nothing compared to what I'm going through in this one. All I had to do in the first fucking war was to kill men, in this war I'm expected to make them. It hasn't been easy, but I haven't done such a bad job, have I? Be honest now, have I? Think of yourselves ten weeks ago and look at yourselves now. Have I done such a bad job? All right, I lose my temper sometimes, and sometimes I go too far. I certainly did this morning, but I don't know what came over me. It hasn't happened before, and it won't happen again, that much I can tell you.

'There's to be an inquiry first thing tomorrow. You'll all be brought up before the CO, and if you shop me, I won't deny it. I may be a fucking brute, but I'm not a fucking liar – '

At which point I felt compelled to cut in: 'Aren't you in fact asking us to lie on your behalf?'

He turned his hard little eyes towards me and looked at me almost pleadingly. 'I'm not asking you to say I didn't do it, all I'm asking you to say is you didn't see it.'

'Doesn't that come to the same thing?'

'No, because in the army you learn not to see a lot, it's part of being a soldier, and if you shop me, I'm done for, finished. The army's my life. I've never done anything else, and I'm too old to try anything new. Message complete.'

He looked round for a response. There was none. He gave me a further look, half-pleading, half-menacing, as if to tell me: 'If I do get the chop I'll know who to blame,' and went out into the night.

'He wants a bayonet up his arse,' said Dad.

'We should have lynched the fucking bugger,' said the Runt.

'If we do shop him,' said Clayton, 'he may be replaced by

someone worse. If we don't, we'll have him eating out of our hands.'

'I'm shopping the bastard whatever happens,' I said, but in the end there was no inquiry, no court-martial and Pike was quietly transferred to another unit.

'The army looks after its own,' said Clayton.

I was outraged and wanted to tell Leibgot to take the matter up with his MP, but he was sent home on sick leave and by the time we met next we were both out of the army and Pike was an unhappy memory.

In the first days of the army, the very condition of strangeness means that everyone is for a while friends with almost everyone else, but gradually cliques begin to form, some based on background, some on locality, some on age, some on disposition. I somehow managed to transcend cliques, possibly because I was not a fully integrated member of any of them.

I was friendly with Leibgot because he was Jewish and otherwise friendless. I was friendly with Clayton because he tended to regard the other men in the hut with mild disdain and believed – mistakenly as it happens – that as somebody with a higher education I shared his feelings. I was friendly with Dad because, while fifteen years his junior, I seemed to be a good bit older and less boisterous than the rest, but, a little improbably, my closest friend of all was the Runt, who was not only small, but thin, with the pointed features, sharp teeth, and restless ways of a ferret.

Most of the men had a good store of obscenities, but somehow when uttered by the Runt they did not seem obscene, if only because he used them so frequently and indiscriminately that they lost all impact.

We all received letters and parcels from home (I with embarrassing frequency) while the Runt received none at all and I sometimes shared my parcels with him, and one afternoon, by way of reciprocity, he offered to take me to a bawdy house, and I felt bound to accept.

I must admit that I was moved less by lust, than by curiosity and, even more, by the desire to fall in with the ways of the crowd. I had learned to swear (which came easily), and to swill beer (which came less easily), to laugh at jokes which I had found unfunny at school, and even to tell them, to join lustily in the singsongs round the NAAFI piano, and I could not for ever abstain from an activity in which all indulged and which was the most frequent subject of conversation.

It was an odd experience walking through a small English country town on a wintry afternoon, with lecherous intent. One did not associate the red-brick Georgian buildings with our mission, nor the small houses built higgledy-piggledy up the steep, cobbled street where the Runt led me. It looked like the setting for a Jane Austen novel.

As we came near the top my step faltered, and not only because of the steepness of the incline.

A few days earlier the MO had shown us a film on syphilis, and the symptoms which he described of its secondary and tertiary stages could have subdued the lust in a satyr. I also had the feeling that if one was doing something one shouldn't, one shouldn't be doing it in broad daylight.

'It's the best time for it, man,' the Runt insisted. 'If you leave it till fucking night they've got half their fucking stuffing fucked out of them.'

'What about the clap?'

'That's why I always go to a fucking pro. They know how to look after themselves, and it's another reason for going early. They're cleaner first thing in the afternoon than last fucking thing at night.'

We were now on the crest of the hill and before us stood a large house with a porticoed doorway and a brass crinolined lady as a doorknocker.

The Runt could hardly contain himself.

'I'm overflowing, man,' he said, and rapped a tattoo on the door which echoed round the empty street. No one answered.

'Let's go,' I said.

'It's a big fucking hoose and they could be on the top fucking flair.'

'The place is obviously empty,' I said, 'and in any case I don't feel like it.'

'Feartie, that's all you are,' he said, 'a big fucking feartie.'

He did not speak to me for the rest of that day, but the incident did not permanently impair our relationship.

It was now nearly Christmas and I was afraid I might be given home leave, and to forestall any such possibility, I told the padre that as a Jew I would be perfectly content to remain in camp over the festival so that others could go.

'That's jolly Christian of you,' he said.

The thought of home was mildly depressing and I wanted to take part in the merrymaking which lay ahead, so that even if I wasn't a Christian, I could, so to speak, be a goy among goyim. As a result I was invited to participate in a pantomime which Clayton was organizing and I showed such promise and inventiveness in the small part he gave me that I was accorded a much larger one and invited to help in revamping the script.

'You really have a flair for comedy,' he said, which was the first time I was complimented on anything other than maths, but while thus engaged I was summoned to take part in quite a different event which had completely slipped my mind, the Jewish festival of *Chanucah*.

Chanucah celebrates the victory of a handful of Jews, the Maccabees, over the Greek invaders of Judea about a century and a half before Christ, and but for *Chanucah* there would have been no Christmas, but I could have done without it that year.

We were summoned to a special service in the camp cinema to be conducted by a visiting Chaplain. I had always thought that I could sense Jews as dog can sense dog, but perhaps the army deprives people of their special scents, for several of the officers, and one of the most loathed of the NCOs, turned out to be Jewish and we filled the cinema to overflowing.

The Chaplain, a lean figure with large glasses and a tiny beard, lit the *Chanucah* candles and led us in singing the familiar *Chanucah* songs which turned out to be less than familiar to about four-fifths of those present, and although I knew them all backwards, I sang them with but half a heart, for I had no wish to be there. I was just beginning to find my place in the larger, more open world, outside, and with those lights, and that Chaplain, and those songs, I felt I was being sucked back into the enclosed world from which I had only just emerged.

Two days later I was in the middle of rehearsal, when I was handed a telegram to say that father was seriously ill.

When I got home he was downstairs in the living room where a bed had been made up for him, fast asleep, with his mouth open. His face was ashen and he reminded me uncomfortably of old Rodgers.

Mother stood beside him wringing her hands.

'He came home one day in a taxi and said, "I don't know what's happening, but I feel like a leaking tyre." His strength began to give out and after a day or two he could no longer walk.'

'Why didn't you call me earlier?'

'What could you have done? We've had doctors, specialists, heart specialists. He's been in hospital for blood-tests and X-rays. They can't find anything. They said he should see a psychiatrist, but you know your father, he'd go mad if I even mentioned it. In the meantime he hardly eats anything, and does nothing but sleep. He doesn't even listen to the wireless.'

'Have you called Sosh?'

She sighed.

'Have you called her?'

'If you ask me that's at the top and the bottom of it all. We've hardly seen anything of her since you left. Remember how it was before? She was home nearly every day, but suddenly she can't get away any more. Corn-harvests, potato-harvests, beet-harvest, but tell me, what do they harvest in November and December? I sent her a telegram two days ago, and her landlady – a very nice woman – phoned back to say she was on leave, so what am I to think? In the meantime Sunny, who is stationed somewhere in the south, he can't tell me where, comes up tearful and broken hearted. She hasn't been answering his letters and he doesn't know what to do. He broke down and cried on my shoulder like a child. I didn't say anything to your father, but he must have guessed. Anyhow that was about the time he took ill.'

I had no doubt that my sister's romance with Sunny was at an end the moment I saw her holding hands with Safran, and I was worried about how my parents, and especially father, would take it, but I never imagined that the effect would be this catastrophic.

I had always regarded Safran with mild dread, as a dark, brooding nemesis, and it seemed as if my instincts were confirmed by events. Sosh was presumably living with him.

I looked at my watch. It was nearly midnight, not the sort of hour at which one could normally phone people, but I couldn't let the matter rest. The only person I knew who might know where I could contact Safran was Theresa Rodgers, and I called her.

The phone rang for some time and I was about to put it down, when an unfamiliar voice answered. It was Edwin.

'I thought you were in Egypt,' I said.

'I was, but am home on sick leave.'

'I'm sorry to hear that. Nothing serious, I hope.'

'Not really, but I take it you're not phoning to ask about my health.' I asked him if he had seen anything of Safran.

'Saw him the other day, as a matter of fact, he was in splendid form.'

'Would you have his phone number?'

'Which one? He's got so many.'

'I'll take them all.'

There were five numbers and (as always happens with me) I reached him with the last.

My name, as I expected, meant nothing to him, until I asked where I could get hold of Sosh. I thought he might deny all knowledge of her whereabouts and I told him right away that father was seriously ill.

'I've no idea where you could get hold of her at this hour of the night,' he said, which I was convinced was a lie, 'but I'll phone around.'

She was no doubt standing, or rather, lying right there beside him, for she phoned back a minute later to say she was catching the first available train. She arrived the next morning looking less than her usual scintillating self.

Father was sitting up in bed being fed porridge by mother when she appeared. At first his mind failed to register her arrival and he continued to sit up with hunched shoulders and sunken eyes, eating his porridge dejectedly.

'Can't you see who's here?', said mother, and it was only then that he took her in, spluttering porridge in all directions, and the light returned to his eyes as she fell upon him with kisses and tears. I had never seen Sosh cry since she was a small child and thought her tear-ducts had atrophied.

The next day was Christmas and by lunch-time father was well enough to join us at table in his dressing-gown, though there was still no colour in his face and he was a bit shaky on his legs. We all spoke at once, as if nervous of letting some embarrassing questions arise, but in a gap in the conversation, father, almost as if speaking to himself, said: 'I suppose it's all over with Sunny.'

'What makes you say that?' asked Sosh.

'It's a feeling I have.'

'We're still very good friends, but he's stationed somewhere in the south, and I'm up in north Wales, so we don't get the chance to meet all that often.'

'Doesn't he even get Christmas off?'

'Wars don't stop even for Christmas.'

'He never even sent me a card.'

'He's Jewish, father.'

'Is he so Jewish that he couldn't send me a Christmas card?'

He was almost his old self.

After lunch Sosh and I went for a walk in a nearby park. It was extremely cold, and misty. The grass was covered with hoar frost and it was slippery underfoot. The mist thickened till the setting sun was a golden blurr.

Sosh put her arm through mine and we walked in silence for a time.

'What do I do?' she asked.

'It *is* all over with Sunny, isn't it?'

'Of course.'

'Can't say I'm surprised. I knew it was over the moment I saw you with Safran. How long have you known him?'

'Safran? Since Pippa's ball.'

'Presumably you've been seeing him since?'

'As a matter of fact I haven't, though I've often thought about him.'

'And he remembered you from that ball?'

'Don't sound so surprised, I'm not all that forgettable. Besides, he had good cause to remember me. We slept together.'

She said it in such a casual, matter-of-fact way that I wasn't sure if I had heard her right, and I stopped to look her in the face.

'*Slept* together? How old were you then, fifteen?'

'Sixteen, nearly seventeen, but it's all right, he wasn't the first. You were precocious mentally, I was precocious physically.'

'It's getting better and better, isn't it? Good God, I wonder if father had even an inkling of what sort of little girl he had on his hands.'

'He didn't, and still doesn't, but mother did. I was fifteen or sixteen at the time and thought I was pregnant and she kept feeding me quinine and giving me hot baths, but it turned out to be a false alarm. I don't suppose you remember, but you kept complaining there was never any hot water in the house. Didn't have a clue, did you? You were such an eager little beaver, always buried in your books.'

'All things considered it's perhaps as well that I was buried in my books. Any other little surprises up your sleeve? Lesbianism perhaps? Bestiality? How do you pass your time in the Welsh hills?'

'You sound surprised and hurt.'

'If I am, it's not because I'm jealous, so let's get that out of the way, or even because I had any illusions about your innocence, but because I thought you had a certain amount of self-respect.'

She looked at me for a moment, her breath emerging in steamy spurts in the gathering dusk.

'It never occurred to me that you were such an odious little prig,' she said, 'but then I don't suppose it's ever occurred to you that I was such a whore. It's a good man who knows his own sister. I don't know what sort of experience you've had, if any. Have you been out with a girl at all?'

'*In* you mean, surely.'

'You know what I mean. I don't suppose you have. You've still got a Victorian view of womanhood. Victorian? I meant Arthurian. Well, you've got a few surprises coming your way, my boy, pleasant ones I hope.'

I asked if she was living with Safran.

'On and off as occasion permits, which is not very often. Wales is a long way from London, especially north Wales.'

'I can't understand how somebody who could love Sunny could fall for someone like Safran.'

'I didn't love Sunny, but saw him through the eyes of people who did, and, of course, he is lovable, which Safran is not. He's arrogant, possessive, bad tempered, conceited, and we quarrel all the time, but I can't see myself settling down with anyone else.'

'Has snobbishness got nothing to do with it? He's an officer, after all, and a gentleman, of good family – '

'He's anything but a gentleman, and his father, to use his own words, was a Levantine shyster, but he does have pots of money, which makes him an aristocrat of sorts, and he's certainly got style.'

'Have you ever brought him home?'

'Never.'

'A pity, because father would take to him, especially in uniform.'

'So I marry Safran, put father on his feet, and Bob's your uncle.'

'That's about it.'

'There's only one thing which hasn't occurred to you. The bastard's already married.'

CHAPTER SIX

It was a quiet wedding.

Sosh was in white, Sunny was in uniform, and father was in tears.

When Sosh came home with the news that she and Sunny had decided to marry, father's first intention was to hire the banqueting suite of the Midland Hotel, which suggested that if he had been cured of one ailment, he had succumbed to another, and it was Sosh who settled the matter. She wanted something small, quick and informal, with the minimum of guests, the minimum of fuss, and no speeches.

Father was aghast. 'No speeches?' he said, as if a marriage without speeches was unconsummated. 'I've got to say a few words for a start. God in heaven, if I can't speak at my own daughter's wedding, when can I speak, and the Rabbi will want a few words – '

'Forget it,' said Sosh, 'we'll marry in a registry office,' and so there were no speeches, but, on father's insistence – and this from a man who only a few months before had thought of himself as an atheist – they were eventually married in an Orthodox synagogue, and I tried to avoid my sister's eye as, in the course of the marriage service, the Rabbi droned on about the chastity and virtues of the daughters of Israel.

There were about fifty guests in all, including about half a dozen soldiers from Sunny's unit, who got rather boisterous and carried both the bride and the groom round on their shoulders.

Father invited two workmates from his factory, including a foreman, a large red-faced man with watery blue eyes, dressed in a brown suit, red tie and black bowler hat, who found the whole affair slightly confusing. In synagogue he took his hat off, and was asked to put it on. In the reception he put his hat on, but everyone had theirs off, so he kept putting his hat on and off all afternoon.

'Grand man, your dad,' he said to me. 'If it weren't for him, half of us wouldn't know what was happening in't war.'

Father was very secretive about the exact nature of his employment and would still answer inquiries with 'careless talk costs lives', or 'walls have ears'. When, after a drink or two I put the same question to the foreman, he said: 'There's nowt wrong wi' asking, but telling would be telling.' His colleague, however, was much more forthcoming: 'Didn't he tell you? He's stores controller in't canteen.'

By 1943, rationing had reached a point where it was difficult to rustle up drinks or dainties even for a wedding. The American contingent had arrived with a caseful of whisky, but if father was stores controller at his factory canteen, he did not use his office to obtain any benefits and, a little unusually at a Jewish wedding, there was more to drink than to eat.

When Malka and Kate left our house that memorable night, they had fled to Blackpool where Malka, using money from the War Damage Commission for the loss of her own house, had opened a small boarding-house. We hadn't seen them since they left, but at mother's insistence – and when mother insisted not even Sosh disagreed – we sent them an invitation and, a little to our surprise, they both came, Malka still harbouring the resentment with which she left, Kate, smiling and mischievous. At twelve she was fully my height, as she proved when she put her back against mine. I might have asked her to do the same with her front, had we not been in company. She no longer looked a child, and no longer behaved like one. Sosh must have been the same at her age.

The Rodgers family had been invited, but Theresa wrote that she would be unable to attend because it was impossible to get reliable nurses for her husband, and she could no longer leave him. Pippa was in Malta, but Edwin turned up in mufti with a little dark-haired girl called Carole, whom he introduced as his fiancée, and who enunciated every word she uttered as if she was performing an elocution exercise.

'Oh, so you're Sammy,' she said, 'Edwin told me so much about you,' which made me wonder what he could possibly have told her, till she went on to address Malka in much the same words.

I drank rather a lot because I always found family occasions something of a strain, and I had hoped to get at least a glimpse of Theresa and was deeply disappointed when she had failed to turn up. I had clearly not purged her from my system as completely as I thought.

Father was in his element; tall, rather distinguished looking, he went among his guests with glass in hand, laughing, slapping backs, greeting friends, and kissing hands in the manner of a Polish gentleman. Mother was also smiling, but looked slightly apprehensive. She knew nothing of my conversation with Sosh when we were home over Christmas, but she had a way of knowing everything, even when she was told nothing.

About a week after I had returned to camp, I received a telegram from Sosh to say that she and Sunny were to be married. I was so used to associating the little yellow envelopes which carried telegrams with bad news that I found it difficult to regard this particular missive as good news, especially as I could imagine the frame of mind in which she had made her decision.

She had told me that Safran was separated from his wife – they had only been together a few months – and was talking about a divorce, and I presumed that she had travelled down to London, demanded to know what was happening and, having failed to obtain satisfaction, she had turned to Sunny. I found it difficult to think of my sister, whose life had hitherto been totally devoted to her own, and only her own, happiness, in the role of dutiful daughter, and I was not entirely convinced that she was doing the right thing, for if she was marrying Sunny for the sake of father, she was not only hazarding her own happiness, but that of Sunny.

If Sosh had any misgivings about her action, no one at the wedding would have known it, for she was a happy and radiant bride, and the only fact which made me suspect that she was not, perhaps, as happy as she looked, was the abandoned way in which she kissed and embraced everyone she encountered, and worked herself up to such a momentum that she even found herself embracing Aunt Malka (who did not, however, thaw at her touch, and continued to move about the place like a dark iceberg).

As for Sunny, half-drunk with whisky, and wholly drunk with happiness, he staggered around behind her, beaming with pride, and saying to all and sundry: 'Ain't she something!'

They had taken a small terrace house in Salisbury, near the Cathedral Close which would have been less than an hour from my base, but my basic, or the 'boy-scout' jamboree' phase of my army life (as one of the officers put it), was now over, and I was home on leave awaiting further orders, which proved very convenient as far as the wedding was concerned, but though the wedding had come (and gone) my orders had not. It had been nice to recover the almost forgotten pleasure of reading late in bed at night, and lying in late of a morning, and soaking slowly in the bath, and going to the pictures in the afternoons, all of which, however, soon began to pall.

And if the pleasures were palling, the pains were becoming acute. Father had been slow to shift his allegiances from the Soviet Union to America because he found it difficult to get excited about anything which happened in the Pacific, especially as the events were usually disastrous, but once Sunny came into his life he began to acquire an American accent, and to pepper his language with American expressions, the meaning of which he barely understood. He stopped twiddling his radio buttons of an evening to pick up the news in Russian, or Polish, or German, or Serbo-Croat – which at least had the virtue of variety – but fixed it on to the American Forces Network, and left it there, and I tired both of the chummy, smooth talk of the programme presenters, and the grave portentousness of the commentators, and we sometimes had altercations when I tried to tune in to the BBC.

Moreover, now that Sosh had finally flown the nest, father focused his attentions upon me. 'When I was your age,' he said, 'I had a wife, I had a business, I nearly had a family. The war's not going to go on for ever. What'll you do when it's finished?'

In the meantime I had no idea what I would be doing while it was still on, and as week succeeded week without a call to arms, I began to think that I was either so rare a property that they couldn't make up their minds as to how best to use me, or so useless as to be unemployable, though the fear which came most frequently to mind was that they had simply forgotten about me, and that I, Private Hoch Samuel, had fallen through a crack in their filing system.

I was cheered by a letter from Clayton, who appeared to be in a similar situation. 'I feel like a small-bit player who is constantly being overlooked by casting directors and agents,' he wrote. 'It's become a matter of "you don't contact us, we'll contact you".'

One Sunday afternoon father went to a funeral and returned in a state of distress for reasons which had nothing to do with the funeral. He had bumped into Krieger who had told him that his son was an officer.

'He didn't win a scholarship to Manchester Grammar School,' he said, 'he didn't win no prizes. He didn't go to University, and didn't get a first-class honours. How is it possible that he is an officer and you're not?'

'Because he's been over three years in the army, and I've only been in three months.'

'You mean they're going to make you an officer now?'

'I don't know.'

'What do you mean you don't know. In the Polish army they made you an officer if you could hold a book the right way up.'

'I am not in the Polish army,' and even as I said that I felt a slight stirring in my heart, as if I had just given a cue to malignant fate.

It would have been shattering enough to have been assigned to a Polish unit the moment I was called up, but after all those months under English skies, amid British troops, 'somewhere in England,' responding to English curses, bending to English drills, marching to English tunes, I felt that I had been finally grafted to the trunk of olde England, integrated, assimilated, at one with the men around me, to the point almost of resenting the Jew in me. And now, suddenly, I was reclassified as a foreigner.

I protested, of course, but with little vehemence, for I was, after all, a soldier, and British enough to have been imbued with the 'ours, not to reason why,' philosophy. The one thought on which I seized at that terrible moment was that if my assignment was due to my Polish birth, I would have been assigned to the Polish army the moment I was called up, and the fact that I was being so assigned only now, suggested a secondment for special duties, which was indeed the case. They, however, turned out to be a good deal more special than I could possibly have imagined.

In the meantime I was ordered to proceed to King's Cross to catch the midnight train to Perth.

I had always loved railway stations, even small local ones with an up and down line, and a tiny bookstall, while railway termini were something of a paradise for me, but King's Cross that night, represented a sort of hell. Long, grimy locomotives sending up huge clouds of steam. Loudspeakers crackling endlessly and sending out announcements which were both unintelligible and inaudible. Mounds of baggage, and troops everywhere, some in regular columns, most in milling crowds, all heavily laden, shouting, pushing, gesticulating, and here and there some stray civilians trying to thrust their way through the heaving mass.

The station was dimly lit and, but for the red-capped military police, and some occasional Americans in white helmets (or 'snow-drops' as they were called), everyone and everything seemed black or grey. One tended to lose all sense of individual identity in the crowd and I had to keep reminding myself who I was, what platform I was making for, and where I was going. There were moments when I in fact lost control and found myself being carried along by the tide, and when I eventually managed to struggle to the right platform, I held on to a lamp-post in case I should be swept away again.

My train was an hour late, which was perhaps just as well, for I would never have got near it if it had arrived on time. It was full, but, as the saying went, 'there's always room on a troop-train', and I somehow managed to clamber aboard with all my kit. Once on, however, it was quite impossible to move in any direction, and anyone anxious to relieve himself, had to wait till the train stopped – which it did frequently – for a rapid descent to the line.

The fact that King's Cross was so full, and so many of us were moving northwards, gave rise to speculation that an invasion of Holland or Norway was at hand and I could sense the tremor of excitement running through the troops around me.

There must have been considerable damage on the line, for we were being shunted back and forth. I fell asleep on my feet, kept upright by the somnolent figures around me, and when I awoke about an hour later we still had not left the outer London area.

It was daylight by the time we reached York, from where we began to make rapid progress until, on the approaches to the Scottish border, we slowed down, stopped and were directed into a siding to let an express roar past. It was a long train pulled by two engines spitting fire and smoke, cutting through the morning mists like a knife, with troops leaning out of every window, shouting obscenities, cheering, gesticulating.

'Now *they're* heading for action,' said a portly figure beside me, which somehow left me with the feeling that he and I were heading for the knacker's yard, and I felt a pang of envy and regret so powerful that I almost doubled up. That wait in the sidings in the cold morning light, while the men of action thundered past on the main line, seemed to symbolize my destiny.

When I alighted in Perth some twelve hours later I was greeted by two uniformed figures, one of them bearing a clip-board. They saluted and I saluted, then the clip-board wallah read out something which sounded like a speech, the only part of which I could make out was my name.

'Don't you speak English?' I said.

'Don't you speak Polish?' said the clip-board carrier.

'No, not a word.'

They looked at each other dumbfounded as me, for the absurdity of the whole situation had suddenly come home to me.

Once I had reconciled myself to my new posting, I had a vague idea that the Polish unit would be but a British unit with a different shoulder-flash, but it was now clear that I had been press-ganged into a foreign army. If I had had any presence of mind, I might have said, 'Look chaps, there's been some mistake, I'm going back to my depot,' but I was too weary and confounded even to protest and I went along with them, one to the left of me, one to the right of me, like a man on a charge.

We drove through the night over narrow, snow-covered mountain passes until a tall, pinnacled building loomed out of the darkness. As we came nearer I could make out a large encampment of Nissen huts on what must have been private parkland.

I was led into the main building itself, down a stone staircase into what looked like a dungeon. It was, in fact, a tiny, white-washed cell with a slit of a window high up in the wall, and a small camp-bed in the corner. The door was not locked behind me, but when I was left on my own I felt like a prisoner, and I sat down on my bed wondering what I had done to bring this on myself.

I was wakened the next morning by a corporal. I couldn't imagine that he didn't know English, but he insisted on addressing me in Polish, and when I stood there shrugging my shoulders in helpless bewilderment, he raged at me for a full minute, which did, at least, offer the comforting thought that NCOs were NCOs, whatever the army. He however calmed down sufficiently to summon a sergeant who, in English, asked me to follow him.

We climbed up one steep spiral staircase, then another, and a third, and a fourth, and I grew dizzier and dizzier with every turn until he opened a door and we emerged from what presumably had been the servants' quarters into the more ornate part of the building, and we moved along a wide, panelled corridor lined with pictures of Highland scenes, and finally I was led into a large room.

'You wait here till somebody come,' said the sergeant, enunciating each word carefully, as if addressing an idiot.

I felt reassured by the proportions of the room, the panelled walls, the carpeted floor, the tall windows, and the magnificent view of distant, snow-capped hills. It was obviously the room of a person of some importance and I again began to feel that I was here not through some caprice of fortune, but for special duties, but then as I looked around me, my heart sank. I noticed a line of Hebrew prayer-books on a shelf and, in a corner, a velvet curtain with gold Hebrew lettering on what looked like a portable ark. I was obviously in some sort of makeshift synagogue.

A minute later the sergeant reappeared followed by a much larger red-faced figure in officer's uniform.

I jumped to my feet and stood there transfixed. I recognized the red, sweaty, pock-marked face, even though it was now beardless, but I could not associate it either with the setting or the uniform.

'You haven't changed a bit,' he said.

I opened my mouth to reply, but no word came.

It was Holtzhacker.

CHAPTER SEVEN

'Take a chair while I get you a drink,' he said, 'you look a bit shaky.'

I sat down and he poured me a glass of whisky from a bottle he kept behind some volumes of the Talmud.

'When I saw your name on the intake of Jewish conscripts I couldn't believe it was you, but I looked through your papers and behold it was. What the hell are you doing in the Polish army?'

I thought I could believe my eyes, but I wasn't at all sure if I could believe my ears, for if this was indeed Holtzhacker, it didn't in the least sound like him. When he vanished eight or nine years ago he may have had a reasonable command of English but, as far as I could recall, it was the halting, uncertain, accented English of the foreigner, with a foreign inflection to his tone, and a foreign arrangement to his words, but now, though one could still discern a slight foreign accent, he had acquired the self-confident resonance and the pukka expression of the officer class. It was as if he had purged his very soul of his old self and had acquired the soul, or at least the sound, of an English gentleman.

I gulped down the whisky.

'Is that better?'

'A bit.'

'To repeat my question, what are you doing in the Polish army.'

I was not sure how to answer, not only in what words, but what tone, for I was, after all, in the presence of a superior officer with three pips on each shoulder, and I was a respecter of pips. On the other hand, I was also in the presence of a fraud who only a few years previously had walked out on his wife and child, to say nothing of his holy congregation, and who, moreover, knew that I knew him for what he was. I was not, I thought, particularly censorious by nature. Most men would have walked out on Malka, and some would have done it sooner, but if I forgave him then, it was partly because I was sorry for him, but now that he had surfaced without his beard and in the full panoply of an officer, I felt free to disapprove.

'I am curious to know what you're doing here at all,' I said. 'Many people think you're dead.'

'Oh, but I am, or at least Holtzhacker is, very dead. You are now in the presence of Rabbi Gilchrist, Chaplain to the Polish forces, and you will be saving me, yourself, and your family, a great deal of trouble if you could put Holtzhacker out of your mind. The poor man died a thousand times and is richly entitled to his rest.'

'Forgive me, but why did you vanish so suddenly?'

'Impulse, dear boy, impulse. I was walking to synagogue on a beautiful summer's evening, when I suddenly asked myself, what are you, Holtzhacker, doing in the black garb of a Rabbi? I had asked myself the same question before, many a time, but you weren't Barmitzvah yet, and I felt that I at least had to see you through to manhood, but once I had done my duty I felt free of further obligations. What business have you with synagogues? I asked myself. You became a Rabbi to get a bread ticket, but it doesn't mean you have to remain a Rabbi for life. And instead of continuing to synagogue, I turned into a side street, where there lived someone I had befriended, or rather, had befriended me – let's say we befriended each other – and we went on to France where we found work in the home of an English gentleman, and where I prospered like Joseph in the house of Potiphar, but then came the war and I was swept up with the Poles, and landed here with what was left of the Polish army, a soldier of misfortune.'

'You left Manchester because you couldn't stand being a Rabbi, yet what are you now if not a Rabbi?'

'But a Rabbi mit pips on,' he said, putting on a Yiddish accent. 'It was the only way of becoming an officer. Yes, I'd much rather have been a gunnery officer. I like guns, big guns, but I didn't have much choice in the matter. It was either the chaplaincy or the ranks. It's only a temporary wartime arrangement. You could call it my contribution to the war effort.'

'And where do I fit into all this, if I may ask?'

He looked at me over his glasses for a moment. 'Do I detect a note of displeasure in your voice?'

'Not displeasure, just confusion. What am I doing here?'

'What are any of us doing here? If you have to be in the army at all, there are some advantages to being in the Polish army. The Pole's at his best as a soldier, especially in the field. The army was about the only thing in Poland which worked. Take Pilsudski – '

'God, not Pilsudski!'

'What's wrong with Pilsudski?'

'Don't tell me you were also in the Polish cavalry?'

'Why? Who was in the Polish cavalry?'

'Father says he was.'

'Your father? In the Polish cavalry? What as? A horse? He wasn't in the cavalry, he wasn't in the infantry. He was press-ganged for a time into a labour battalion, but whether it was by the Russians or the Germans or the Poles, I don't know, and I doubt if he knew himself. There was such chaos at the time, nobody knew what was happening. There is one thing I will say for him, though, he stayed alive. Most people I knew didn't. This war's a picnic compared to the last. You can't imagine the chaos. There were people moving in all directions, but in parts of Poland you could change nationality two or three times a year merely by stopping in the one place. You didn't know who you were, what you were, or where you were.'

'I'm beginning to feel a bit like that myself.'

'You, my boy, are sitting pretty because, as you'll find out, I've got you the cushiest billet in the army.'

'*You* got me?'

'How else? Do you think Sikorski sent for you? I don't know how you happened to be in the Polish army after you were conscripted into the British one, but I assure you it's no pleasure for a Jew to be in the Polish army. It certainly wasn't in Poland, and it's not much of a joy even here – at least in the ranks, which is why I became a Chaplain. As you know, I've taken a close interest in your progress ever since you were a boy and when I saw your papers I got two surprises, the first that you were in the Polish army at all, the second that you were not on an officer's course, but if I can't offer you a commission, I can offer you the next best thing. There are nearly two hundred Jewish lads in this camp, and they can be quite a handful. Jews can be awkward and Poles can be awkward, but there is no one quite as awkward as a Jewish Pole, unless it's a Polish Jew.'

'In other words, you want me to be your acolyte.'

'Exactly.'

'Supposing I said no?'

'You'd be a bloody fool if you did, and an ungrateful one at that. You can't imagine the trouble I went to and the strings I pulled to get you here. I almost had to go as far as Sikorski. And it's not only that. When I buried Holtzhacker and became Gilchrist, I buried all the remnants of my past. I've got new papers, a new identity, I'm a new man, and I had to think twice before bringing up someone who would be a living reminder of Holtzhacker, and yet you're looking at me, and talking at me, as if I've done you a great wrong. There's an old Yiddish saying, "People will forgive you the wrongs you've done them, but never the favours." You'll have your own room, with your own bed, with even a light above your bed, and your own kettle and gas-ring. No guard duties, no pack-drill, no kit-inspection, no marches, no bull, though, of course, you'll have to look reasonably decent, which, as far as I remember, you always did. You'll be moving mainly among officers and hardly mixing with the other ranks – '

'I don't mind the other ranks.'

'What do you know about other ranks?'

'I did my basic training with them.'

'They're schoolboys in the British army, smutty stories, naked pin-ups, ribald laughter and weak beer. It's all a big joke, or at least they treat it like one. They've got less to laugh at in the Polish army, first of all because they've lost their country; second, because they're cut off from their families; third, because they're older, and worst of all, because they're religious fanatics – on their knees half the time, and crossing themselves the other half. And when they do get merry, it's not on watery beer, but on the strongest poison they can find, and even then, they don't get merry, but maudlin, and cry themselves to sleep. There's nothing to match a Polish soldier in action, but in the barracks he's a different kettle of fish. You'd go out of your mind in the ranks. But in any case, why am I talking to you as if I'm trying to sell you something? You're in the bloody army now, boy, and you're here under orders.'

I automatically jumped to my feet at this sudden bark of authority, but he told me to sit down again.

'I take it you haven't changed your religion or anything like that, you're still Jewish?'

'Not as Jewish as I used to be – Sir.'

'That's all to the good. Your predecessor, a man called Peshkin, who seemed to be perfectly normal when I took him on, turned out to be a religious fanatic, and forgot not only that he wasn't in Poland, but that there's a war on. He kept digging up obscure feasts and fasts, which were rarely observed even in Poland, for special services, and demanded that I organize kosher this and kosher that, when the Chief Rabbi had already said that the dietary laws didn't apply to men on active service. We were lucky to have food at all, but he wasn't happy with anything they served up and got hold of a barrel of salt herrings and lived on that, which I wouldn't have minded if he hadn't stank the place out.'

I was able to assure him that I was not that particular.

I returned to my cell and sank down on my bed in a daze. I had no idea what to make of it all, but in time two things became clear. The first was that in spite of Holtzhacker's desire to bury the past (I could never learn to think of him as Gilchrist), he wanted someone around to see him in his hour of triumph with those pips on his shoulders. He was like the Jew who stayed away from synagogue on Yom Kippur to play golf, and holed in one, whereupon he put his hands to his face. 'Oh, God,' he said, 'who can I tell?'

The second reason was that if he had to have an acolyte, which he clearly did, I was the safest man to have around, if only because anyone else might see through him. Not that I didn't, but then, of course, I already knew him for what he was; knew him so well, in fact, as to be almost implicated in his masquerade, so that there was little danger of exposure and, to limit the danger further, he kept me isolated in my little cell in the main building.

It was, as he said, a cosy billet, and I was never averse to comfort, but I was not particularly happy in my new role, for if I had to be in the army, of whatever nationality, I wanted to be a soldier like other soldiers, and not a superannuated altar-boy.

I was attached to an artillery brigade and, whatever Holtzhacker may have said about them, the Poles were an impressive body of men, rather short of stature, but seasoned, lean, tough and on parade they moved as a man. It was a pleasure to watch them. They were real soldiers, and I felt I was being denied the opportunity of being among them. I could understand the yearnings which gave rise to father's cavalry fantasies.

There was the sound of trumpets at dawn, the bark of orders, the rapid clatter of boots on concrete, the rush of dispatch riders, the movement of vehicles, and the thunder of guns in the distant hills, all of which passed me by, and I felt like a child who had been invited to a party without being allowed to join in the games.

One evening Holtzhacker asked me to serve in the officers' mess. He made it seem like a privilege, but he obviously wanted me to see with my own eyes the exalted circles in which he moved. I was duly impressed.

The mess was in a large panelled hall lined with portraits of white-haired figures alternating with stags' heads, and the stags looked a good deal more cheerful than the portraits, but the scale of the room and its loftiness dwarfed everyone in it, so that even Holtzhacker looked small. The officers were immaculately turned out, with knife-edge creases and gleaming leather, and never a hair out of place, but few of them were much taller than me, while the commander, Brigadier Maclutzynszky, who Holtzhacker usually referred to as Mac, a slight, bald-headed figure with wire-rimmed glasses and a bushy moustache, was, if anything, smaller than me, but his campaign ribbons, or 'gravy stains', as we called them, covered about half his tunic. He had a legendary reputation for his ferocity and courage, and some of his medals, I was told, were gained fighting with the Austro-Hungarian army against the British in the Balkans in the first world war. He had later served under Pilsudski in the cavalry against the Russians, and I almost asked if he had ever come upon one Nathan Hoch in the course of his service. He did not look particularly fierce that evening, with his eyes sparkling behind large glasses, but he seemed to crackle with energy and had a presence out of all proportion to his size, and it seemed to me then that the measure of a man lay within him, and one was only small if one felt oneself to be small.

I cannot say that I felt particularly large that evening, for the Polish officers were very much like their English counterparts and, certainly at a social gathering, did not allow the other ranks to impinge upon their consciousness and I and the other stewards moved among them like ghosts. At first I thought I was being wilfully ignored, but then it occurred to me that one could acquire a habit of looking at people without seeing them.

Holtzhacker, on the other hand, was in his element. Mac was obviously very fond of him, as were two or three of the other senior officers and although I had the feeling that they regarded him as a sort of court jester, I could not help admiring the ease with which this uncouth son of an impoverished ghetto family, moved among the most exalted names in Poland, names, which I was given to understand, were the Polish equivalent of the Cecils, the Cavendishes and the Howards, which did not, however, mean that I actually warmed to him.

I had been with him now for nearly two months, and, much as no man is a hero to his valet, no priest is sacred to his acolyte, and Holtzhacker verged on the profane.

I was, among other things, his driver and every now and again I had to take him into Perth for what he called a conference. He made it sound like a diocesan meeting, but the very fact that I was always required to drop him some distance from his venue – 'I need the exercise,' he kept telling me – left me in little doubt as to the nature of the exercise or with whom he was conferring, and I was surprised that, knowing full well that I knew him full well, he still felt the need to resort to subterfuge.

Then there was the time when a Perth distillery was raided and some cases of whisky stolen. A large detachment of military police descended on the camp with a fine-tooth comb and found all sorts of improbable objects, but no whisky. Some days later, however, I was preparing the Ark for our weekly service, when I found twelve bottles stacked among the holy scrolls of the law.

'I meant to tell you,' he said, 'we've got *Purim* coming up and I laid by a small store.'

Purim is one of the two occasions in the Jewish calendar when one is actually enjoined to make merry, but I asked him if the holy Ark was the right place to store aids to merriment.

'Why not?' he said. 'There's nothing profane about whisky, especially a good malt. I use it for sacramental purposes.'

And yet he could preach, and preach convincingly, about the virtues of chastity and probity and look me full in the face without batting an eyelid, but I found it difficult to disapprove of him. Did one's critical faculties atrophy with age or army service, or was I merely overwhelmed by the sheer brazenness of the man?'

We sometimes relaxed together last thing at night with tumblers of malt in our hands, and I asked him how he came by a name like Gilchrist.

'I wanted to shrug off Holtzhacker for good and bury him without trace, so that there was no point in becoming a Holtz or a Hacker, or even a Wood or a Chopper. If you have to change your name don't go in for half-measures, don't mess about with translations, or rumps, but change it completely, and, as a mark of respect to my employer, I adopted his name.'

'Didn't he mind?'

'He might have done, but he died. A fine old English gentleman.'

'The name's Scottish.'

'Which doesn't surprise me. The finest English gentlemen are Scotsmen.'

He was careful, even in his most relaxed moments, never to ask about my family, presumably out of fear that if we touched on mine, it might lead on to his. I could understand why he wished to have no reminder of Malka, but I marvelled at his lack of curiosity about his own child. I would have liked to tell him what a beautiful girl she had become, but I learned to abide by the rules of the game and to treat his past as past.

Even with the pips on his shoulders, he continued to have misgivings about the nature of his calling.

'There are nearly two hundred Jewish boys in this camp, self-confessed Jews that is, and when we come together for prayers I sometimes feel like telling them: "What the hell are you waiting for? Now's your chance, you stupid bastards. There's a war on and everybody's mixing with everyone else. No questions asked about what you were, it's what you are that counts, and if you're a good enough soldier, you're forgiven everything, even your Jewishness. You'll never get another opportunity like this. This is your chance to turn goy, to get lost for good." Instead I keep prattling on about their being links in the golden chain of tradition, and I sometimes have a horrible feeling that many of them take me seriously.'

'Why don't you take your own advice and make a private getaway?'

'God knows I've tried, but he must have a soft spot for me, because every time I make a break for it, he whips me back in. In any case, as long as you have people persisting in being Jewish, you've got to have people to look after them. And you must admit, I'm doing a pretty good job. Anybody can be a Rabbi, but to be a Rabbi, and a successful Rabbi, when you don't believe a word of what you're saying, takes a bit of doing.'

It was me, in fact, who – preaching apart – performed most of his holy offices. It was customary for the Jewish troops to dine together after the service on Friday nights, and I took pains to get hold of white tablecloths, white bread, flowers and kosher wine, to give a festive look to the dining room, and also, if only for that one meal, kosher food which arrived pre-cooked from Glasgow, so that even the most devout members of the brigade could enjoy it. We also had hot soup prepared under my supervision, to make sure that it too was kosher.

We had Mac as a guest at our table one Friday and he said

that if he could be assured of such a meal every week, he would turn Jewish, which might have been gratifying but for the fact that he went down with a stomach complaint the next day.

Holtzhacker regarded my efforts with approval on the one hand, and apprehension on the other, for he was beginning to fear that I had the makings of another Peshkin, and his fears were not wholly misplaced, for the more immersed I became in my holy duties, the more I enjoyed them. I, who only a few months earlier had been revelling in my first experience of goymanship, was becoming a Rabbi by contagion, purveyor to the faithful and defender of the faith.

I had never felt there was anything inherently superior in being a Jew or, for that matter, in being a goy, but I had found the condition of goyishness less oppressive and more fun. God was a little too omnipresent in Jewish life and he tended to cramp one's style. On the other hand a Jew among Jews was on home ground, while a Jew among goyim felt a little like a guest and was under some constraint to behave. Everything had its advantages, and everything had its drawbacks, but what I hated was the sensation of dangling between the two, and I began to wonder whether I should finally reconcile myself to my Jewishness and leave it at that.

I had lacked the courage to tell my father in person that I had been posted to the Polish army, but when I wrote to him, he treated the matter with surprising equanimity.

'It can only mean one thing,' he wrote, 'they want to make you an officer,' and, a little later, I was, indeed, promoted, though only to the rank of corporal.

I missed the companionship I had enjoyed during my basic training. I wasn't sure if the soldiers around me were ignorant of English, but they made it a rule to speak only Polish, and while the Jewish troops did occasionally resort to Yiddish (which I knew fairly well), they quickly switched to Polish, when I was around, which suggested that I was not quite trusted.

I not only slept away from the other ranks, I washed away from them, which was important, for there is nothing like a shower-room to reduce people to essentials and induce a sense of camaraderie. Nor was I subjected to the usual rigours of army life, all of which set me apart from my fellows, but I did eventually become friendly with a thick-set, dark-haired figure with horn-rimmed glasses called Itzkovitch, who was something of an intellectual, something of a poet, something of a revolutionary, and, as events were to show, more than something of a nuisance, and he told me that I was generally regarded as the Chaplain's nark.

I was more surprised than offended and asked him what there was to nark about.

'The Poles don't trust us, didn't you know?'

'From what I know of the army,' I said, 'nobody is trusted, and with good reason.'

'Yes, but we're specially distrusted, and they expect Gilchrist to keep an eye on us.'

Jews have always been suspicious of authority, especially their own, but I nevertheless thought this was a bit much because, whatever Holtzhacker's failings, he showed some concern for the welfare of the Jewish troops, and I listed five recent cases in which he had intervened to have charges against Jewish troops dropped, or to have their sentences reduced.

'Ah,' said Itzkovitch raising a finger, 'but you don't know of the cases where he failed to intervene.'

'Are you suggesting that Jewish troops never get up to tricks, and that if they do they should be allowed to get away with it?'

'Of course not, but in this camp goyim are innocent until they're proved guilty, while Jews are treated as guilty until they're proved innocent. Gilchrist knows that, but he's perfectly happy to play along with the system. He's in with them. In fact he's as good as one of them – you only have to see them together.'

And that, I suppose, was at the root of their suspicion, the fact that he, a Jew, should be acceptable among Poles.

The festival of *Purim* was almost upon us and Holtzhacker asked me to prepare an appropriate entertainment and I asked Itzkovitch if there was any talent among the Jewish troops in the camp.

'Talent?' he said. 'They're bursting with it. Leave it to me.' And a week later he appeared with a whole troupe of actors, singers, dancers, instrumentalists, but his *pièce de résistance* was a parody on army life which he had written himself, and which he handed to me with great pride.

It was of course, in Polish, and I passed it on to Holtzhacker, who tittered over the first page, and giggled over the second. 'Not bad,' he said, 'not at all bad. This could be very amusing,' but then, as he turned another page, his smile faded, his face darkened, his brow furrowed, and he finally threw it to the ground with a loud curse.

'I know you don't read Polish,' he roared, 'but if you entrust something like this to anyone, you should make sure he's got a bit of sense in his head. Who wrote it?'

I didn't answer.

'Was it Itzkovitch? It was, wasn't it? I've a good mind to put him on a fucking charge, the *mamzer*.' The reversion to Yiddish, even more than his tone of voice, gave me the full measure of his wrath.

'Itzkovitch organized it,' I said, 'but I believe it's a co-operative effort.'

'I've had to bear the cross of Itzkovitch since the day I joined the army, in case you don't know. He's a profane Peshkin. Peshkin made trouble in the name of God, while he makes trouble for its own sweet sake. I should have warned you against him. There's enough in here to hang us all. He makes fun of everybody and everything, me included, which I don't mind, but he also makes fun of God – '

'But is that so unusual? It's *Purim* after all.'

'It may be *Purim* for us, but not for them. To us God is almost a member of the family so we can joke about him now and again, but not among Poles. They take their religion seriously. And he doesn't stop with God. He makes fun of the Virgin Mary, of Mac, of Sikorski, of the Polish army. You'd better burn this fucking thing before anyone sees it, though I'd rather burn Itzkovitch first.'

'In the British army – '

'Don't tell me what happens in the British army. You're in the Polish army now and in the Polish army you don't make fun of your superior officers, of God, or the mother of God. I don't know what gets into these bastards. It's not as if all this is for some private little do. Mac takes a particular interest in the welfare of his Jewish troops and always attends these occasions as a matter of courtesy. So does Father Urbansky and the rest. It's like inviting an honoured guest to your house and spitting in his face. Let me give you an example of their sense of humour.'

He picked up the script and opened it at random.

'Listen to this, and remember it's for an audience which includes a Polish Brigadier and a Jesuit Priest: "In the beginning God created the heavens and the earth. And it was a botched job, which is why everybody thinks God was a Pole." Do you think that's funny?'

'Not particularly, at least not in English.'

'It's worse in Polish, and it doesn't improve as it goes on. Would you like to hear what they have to say about the Virgin Mary?'

'I can imagine.'

'And this isn't by youngsters straight out of school, like your British soldiers, it's by grown men. You don't know what I have to put up with these bastards. The Poles are bastards enough, but the Jewish Poles are bastards twice over.'

'But I thought you got on with the Poles like a house on fire.'

'You mean because they fall over themselves to shake my hand and fill my cup, and clap my back with cries of *chlop z wiary*? That's because I'm the resident good Jew, the one they can point to and say some of their best friends are Jews. Do you think I don't know that they wink and laugh behind my back? They're guests here and know they have to be on their best behaviour and, on the whole, they behave well. It's difficult, when you're brought up to believe that the Jews are the killers of Christ and the accursed of God, to treat them as equals, and the Itzkovitches and their like haven't made it any easier for them. The more accommodating the Poles, the more liberties they take. I had a snivelling little rascal the other day who overstayed his leave by seventy-two hours and explained, by way of excuse, that his watch had been stolen. We had another man on a rape charge, one of Peshkin's crowd, a holy man fuming with incense, who claimed he couldn't possibly have done it because he was fasting that day, and that he couldn't get an erection on an empty stomach.'

'Does every Jewish soldier have to be a saint?'

'He isn't, and he's not expected to be, and in fact very few of them get into trouble, but those that do somehow feel that they're victimized if they're caught and that I'm failing in my duties if I can't bail them out. I tell you, what Moses had to go through in the wilderness is as nothing compared to what I have to go through here, and yet when I ask you to organize some light entertainment as a public relations exercise, you come up with this.'

'With respect, as I don't speak Polish, I was hardly the best person to be charged with the task.'

'But as you do speak Yiddish, you should have had some idea who you were dealing with. You can go back to your Bolshie friends and tell them that if this is the best they can do, not only will there be no *Purim* celebrations, they can forget about the extra rations I rustle up for them on Friday nights. They can eat fucking spam like everyone else.'

I took the message to Itzkovitch whose reaction was much as I expected: 'There, what did I tell you? Sucking up to the Polacks as always.'

They did not come back with a more acceptable script and the *Purim* celebrations were cancelled.

What concerned me rather more was the possibility that our Passover celebrations – a month away – might also be cancelled, for something of the gravest importance affecting the entire camp had happened. I had no idea what it was and Holtzhacker, who claimed to be privy to everything, was also in the dark, but everybody was aware that some sort of crisis was brewing. There was a small landing-strip nearby which was normally hardly used, but now senior officers, sometimes accompanied by civilians, seemed to be coming and going on every wind. Mac left hurriedly one morning in a Hurricane which he piloted himself.

We later learned the cause of the commotion. The Germans had dug up the bodies of fifteen thousand Polish officers and men who, they said, had been massacred some years previously by the Russians. Most people at the time treated the reports as German propaganda, but the Poles had ample evidence that they were well founded, and a political crisis ensued, leading to a breach of relations between Moscow and the Polish government in exile.

We, of course, while sensing that something untoward had happened, had no inkling of the scale of the tragedy or its implications, and when Holtzhacker called on Mac's adjutant to discuss Passover arrangements, he bawled him out of his office, and when I used my own initiative to obtain supplies of matzo and other necessities for the eight days of the festival, Holtzhacker, in turn, bawled me out.

'You don't have to cater for every fanatic in the army, don't you know there's a war on? You'll be lucky if you get enough supplies to cover you over the first two days. Nobody's expected to keep the whole of Passover in wartime.'

'Don't the others get special rations over Christmas?'

'Yes, but Christmas lasts one day, and not a bloody week or more. Besides, we also get the Christmas extras. We celebrate their festivals and ours, and want it this way, that way and every way. Well it can't be done, not in wartime.'

'Can't I at least try?'

'If you do, don't expect any help from me. I don't want to know about it. You'd think that all those years at Manchester Grammar School and University would have knocked a bit of sense into your head, but it hasn't. You're worse than Peshkin.'

Early the next morning we were ordered to strike camp. We were electrified with the announcement and the wildest rumours swept the place, including one that we were about to be dispatched to the Far East to open a second front *against the Russians*!

The Poles moved with a new jauntiness to their step and even Holtzhacker acquired the glowing look of a man whose hour of destiny was at hand.

'Ah!' he said, 'action at last, the real war.'

We in fact – for the time being, at least – went no further than Marhill Barracks in Glasgow and it was there that I encountered what, as far as I was concerned, was to be the most important experience of the war.

CHAPTER EIGHT

We arrived in Glasgow three or four days before Passover, which left us with too little time to make our own arrangements for the festival, but with the help of local Rabbis we managed to obtain private hospitality for the two hundred or so Jewish troops in our unit, while Holtzhacker and I were the guests of a Rev. Efrem Pollock.

The Rev. Pollock called to deliver his invitation in person and when I looked at the name on the visiting card and then at the bearer I became afraid that one or the other, or perhaps both, of us had made a mistake, for he had the dog's collar and black attire, even to the little black rosette in the band in his hat, of an Episcopalian divine, and that we were being invited to celebrate Easter rather than Passover. It soon, however, became clear that he was Jewish and that he had called to greet us before the festival so that we should not feel strangers at his table.

He had himself been a Chaplain to the forces and had only recently returned to civilian life after a driving accident which had left him with a slight limp.

'It's enough that we were strangers in Egypt,' he said in a resonant voice, as if addressing us from a pulpit. 'I shouldn't want you to feel strange in Glasgow.'

He lived quite comfortably in a large sandstone house and had about twenty guests at table, including a young woman called Mrs Bannerman. She was nicely formed with a bust which looked a trifle too large for her otherwise slight build, a flawless, dusky complexion, a bright, if toothy, smile, and large dark eyes. She had a small noisy boy at her side whose behaviour forced her to smile apologies in all directions throughout the evening, but she made no attempt to restrain him, and when she smiled at me, I felt as if my soul was about to depart my body. My sole memories of that evening were the eyes and smiles of the mother, and the obstreperous behaviour of the child. Everybody else around them seemed to exist in a haze.

As we walked back to barracks Holtzhacker said to me: 'I was ashamed of you. I was telling Pollock what a brilliant young man you were, with scholarships from here and prizes there, and a first class honours, and you sat there like a dummy with your mouth open, staring at that woman and saying nothing. As a matter of fact there was a very nice young girl sitting right next to you.'

'Was there?'

'A beauty, and you didn't even look in her direction. And you didn't touch the food, even though it was the best meal I've had since the war began. I don't know what they must have thought of you. That's the last time I'm going out for a meal with you my boy.'

He had his coat collar up about his ears and complained bitterly of the cold as we strode briskly through the night, but the air seemed soft to me, even balmy. I took a very long time to undress and when I finally settled into bed I lay awake with my head on the pillow staring into the darkness and seeing every detail of her features, her black hair, her neat little nose (which looked as if it might have been tampered with), the slight obtrusion of her teeth, her dimpled cheeks, the small cleft in her chin, the beginnings of her underchin, but above all, her eyes, large, dark and slightly wanton. Her appearance in general was Italianate rather than Jewish and I saw her almost as a mischievous madonna.

I rushed to synagogue the next morning in the hope of seeing her again and was rewarded with the sight of her in the ladies' gallery with the small boy beside her. She had to take him out during the sermon because he was causing a disturbance, and I slipped out quickly and met her as she was coming down the stairs. I saw her legs before I saw the rest of her, beautifully formed, in elegant shoes.

'Don't you like sermons either?' she said.

'I wanted a breath of fresh air,' I said.

Her son tugged at her skirt. 'Who is this man?' he demanded, 'what does he want from you?'

'This gentleman's a soldier, Jeremy dear, and he's just being sociable.'

'I don't like him.'

'That's very rude, Jeremy darling.'

'Tell him to go back inside.'

She smiled her apologetic smile which by now was almost built into her face. 'His father's been away for two years now, and he's getting to be something of a handful.'

I nodded sympathetically, but at that moment I would have foregone my share of the kingdom of heaven to give the little lad a hard kick.

'I'd better take him home,' she said, 'he's too much of a nuisance to go back inside. Now say goodbye to the gentleman, Jeremy.'

'Shan't.'

About ten days later I was again in synagogue, and we went through much the same routine, only this time she invited me back for lunch. I hesitated if only because I was not too sure whether I could restrain myself from assaulting her son in the course of the meal, but when we got to her house I was confronted with something worse, in the person of her mother, a large woman, with a huge bosom, crumpled face, tinted glasses and ill-fitting dentures.

Over the soup she asked me: 'You any relation to the Hochs of Hartlepool?'

'I shouldn't think so.'

Over meat she asked me if I was any relation to the Hochs of Huddersfield, and got the same reply.

Over pudding she asked: 'You a corporal?'

'I am, for my sins.'

'Hitler was a corporal,' after which she said no more. I saw little of her daughter because Jeremy had decided to eat in his room.

'But Jeremy darling, your food will get cold by the time I bring it upstairs.'

'I like it cold.'

And so she kept rushing up and down the stairs, while I was left to entertain her mother.

A few days later Holtzhacker called me into his inner sanctum and sat behind his desk beaming at me like a full moon.

'I've had two complaints about you, Corporal Hoch, both of a rather unusual order. Shall I read them out to you?'

I was a trifle mystified by it all, and not least by the pleasure he seemed to be getting out of it, for he donned his glasses slowly and ceremoniously and beamed at me over the rims before continuing.

'The first is from the Reverend Pollock and speaks for itself. The second is rather more mysterious. Are you listening?'

'I'm all ears.'

'"Dear Gilchrist. I wonder if my wife or I have done anything to upset the young man ..." et cetera, et cetera. It's rather a rambling affair, so I'll get to the heart of it. "I couldn't help noticing that he hardly touched his food during the entire meal, which my wife thought was a reflection on her cooking, but which I ascribed to other causes. Since then, however, he has been in my synagogue twice and, on each occasion he has made a point of rising from his place and walking out almost as soon as I began my sermon, all of which has left me slightly perplexed, and I wonder, therefore, whether my wife or I have done or said anything to offend him, or whether he objects to the content or tone of my sermon. In either case I would be grateful to know what it could be. One makes enough enemies wittingly without adding to their number through some unwitting offence ..." et cetera, et cetera. How say you, Corporal Hoch, guilty or not guilty?'

'Guilty, I'm afraid. I shall have to write to apologize and explain.'

'But before you do, listen to this. I can't make out the signature, but I think you'll know who it is when I get to the body of the letter, which reads as follows: "My daughter is a respectable married woman, and I don't like it when a soldier who is not even an officer – two things he's got on his sleeve, that's all – keeps telephoning my daughter and bothering her. Hasn't he got a war he can go and fight, a young man like him? My daughter is too kind hearted to complain, but I think as the Rabbi you should know what's happening, and stop it. Her husband, the doctor – he's a specialist, as a matter of fact – is in Egypt, and wouldn't like it either ..."'

He put down the letter and took off his glasses, still beaming.

'It doesn't sound like you, does it? But I spoke to the woman and it's obvious from her description that it couldn't have been anyone else. The two letters are therefore linked, I take it, which is something of a relief. I was getting nervous of the thought of you becoming a regular shul-goer again, specially when your duties don't call for it, but you were looking for Mrs Bannerman, and not God, am I right?'

'With respect, I'm not sure if it's any of your business.'

'But the welfare of Jewish troops in the unit is my business, and so is the good name of the unit.'

I had phoned Mrs Bannerman – or Emma, as I had by now learned to call her – three or four times and, unfortunately, her mother had answered each time (in very brusque tones: 'You the corporal?' 'Yes.' 'She's not in') so that it may have seemed as if I was trying to molest her, but even so, three, or even four, abortive phone calls did not constitute an offence under the King's Regulations, or, for that matter, under General Sikorski's regulations, and even if they did, I did not care for the familiar and patronizing tones in which he addressed me. When he was a broken-down Rabbi in a broken-down synagogue, he treated me as an adult and confidant, but now that our positions were, to an extent, reversed, he treated me like a schoolboy. As he was well aware, I only had to open my mouth to deprive him of his pips and position, but he took my discretion for granted, which I did not resent. What I did resent, however, was that despite the fact that I could shop him, and despite the fact that he deserved to be shopped, he continued to treat me in this way.

'Is it an offence for a soldier to phone a civilian?' I asked.

'Anything a soldier does, or fails to do, can be construed as an offence. Poles are guests in this country, remember, and as Jewish Poles we are guests twice over, so that we have to be doubly discreet. You are also my personal assistant, which makes you a holy man of sorts, and which is yet another cause for discretion. And finally, there is the matter of ethics. Mrs Bannerman is, after all, the wife of a serving officer, which may be no consideration in some forces, but you happen to be in the Polish army, which has a particularly strict code of honour, and conduct which might be unbecoming to an officer in the British army, is unbecoming even to a private in the

Polish one. Oh I know married women have their attractions. They're experienced, they're safe, if their husbands are abroad, they are lonely, and there is only a slight danger of romantic entanglements, but I assure you that apart from all other considerations, you would be wasting your time with this particular piece of goods.'

I was anxious to bring the interview to an end in case I should respond in a manner which most definitely would be a breach of King's Regulations and, standing stiffly to attention, I said: 'Will that be all, Sir?'

'Sir?' he shouted, 'Sir? Don't you talk to me like a soldier on a charge. I've never pulled superior rank on you, so don't you pull subordinate rank on me. I'm talking to you as a friend. You're entitled to a bit of fun, especially in wartime, and more especially as I suspect you've not had all that much fun up to now, but you'll get none with her. You're an intelligent and attractive young man, and you don't have to go sniffing after second-hand goods. I'm talking to you now as man to man, and in down-to-earth terms you'll never get her down to earth.'

In that sense, certainly, I would have been wasting my time, but although I had often conjured up such a situation in my dreams – both by night and by day – I had never seriously entertained any hope of doing so, nor did I feel any particular need to do so. The Runt once told me about a friend who could get drunk on the mere smell of whisky. Well, I could get an orgasm – metaphorically speaking – from the mere sight of a woman, or at least that particular woman, and I only had to hear her voice for my day to be made, which is why I had persisted in my phone calls, but the interview with Holtzhacker left me feeling so unhappy and humiliated that I wondered if I shouldn't follow his advice and try and forget about her.

And I might have done so but for the eruption of spring. There had been no gradual transition from season to season. One day it was winter with grey clouds and cold winds, the next there was blue skies, sunshine, warmth. Glasgow had not suffered as badly as Manchester in the bombing, and although the buildings looked grey and shabby, on a bright day the city took on a continental air, an impression enhanced by the number of continentals, Poles, Frenchmen, Dutchmen, Belgians, to say nothing of Americans and Canadians, one saw about the place, and all of them, it seemed, in the company of the most attractive women. I never in my life felt so alone as I did that day, and kept seeing Emma in every face, until finally I went into a stationers', bought paper and envelopes, and wrote her a note which I dropped into her letter-box. It would, of course, have been simpler to have knocked on the door, but I was afraid of being confronted by her mother or son, or both. I explained that I had tried to phone her, without success, and wondered if she could meet me in a certain restaurant for tea. 'There is no need to reply,' I added. 'I shall be there at four and if you should be able to join me, I shall be delighted to see you. If not I shall take it that you are otherwise engaged.'

I arrived on the dot of four, not daring to hope that she would really turn up, and when she did not appear by twenty past, I ordered tea.

A minute later she was by my table, smiling and apologetic. 'I'm sorry I'm late, but four o'clock is a very awkward time for me.'

I rose, took her hand and kissed it, which was something I had picked up in the Polish army, and she giggled with embarrassment.

'I don't know why you picked this particular place,' she said. 'All my friends come here and God knows what they'll think if they see me, a respectable married woman, with a foreign soldier.'

'I'm not that foreign,' I said.

She sat down and looked at me smilingly. 'When I got your note I couldn't make out the signature so I'm here as much out of curiosity as anything else, but I'm glad it's you. I thought you were cross with me.'

'Why should I be cross with you?'

'Well that lunch was a bit of a fiasco, wasn't it and you didn't phone – '

'Oh, but I did, several times, but obviously your mother didn't pass on the message.'

She sighed. 'My mother's my chastity belt. You wouldn't think so looking at her now, poor dear, but she was a bit of a girl when she was younger, and she thinks I could be up to the same sort of tricks myself. Not much chance of that with her and Jeremy on top of me, is there?'

'Where there's a will there's a way,' I said.

I looked into her eyes and had the distinct feeling that this relationship could be more rewarding than I had allowed myself to believe. My trousers were becoming taut. An acquaintance passed us at that moment and when I rose to be introduced, I had to remain half-sitting, half-standing, to cover my shame.

'See what I mean? Everybody here knows me. My name'll be mud. Once people see you talking to a soldier, they think the rest follows.'

'If only it would,' I said.

She scrutinized my face for a moment, as if not sure how to take that. 'You're not as innocent as you look, are you?' she said.

'People keep saying that. I don't think I look innocent.'

'Oh but you do, it's one of the things I like about you. You obviously don't believe in wasting time, or words, I could see that by your letter. Two or three scrawled lines, about twenty words, almost a telegram. Most people who write to me write screeds and screeds.'

'I'm a mathematician by training, and maths is all shorthand, so that even twenty words is a lot for me. I believe in getting and keeping to the point.'

'So that – to get to the point – this is in the nature of a seduction tea.'

She said it all with a smile so that even if her tone seemed disapproving, her eyes were not.

'One normally goes in for seduction dinners,' I said, 'but what with wartime shortages and all that, one has to settle for tea.'

'You must think I'm easy meat. Young woman, probably lonely, husband overseas. All you have to do is to get her on her own and you're home and dry – if dry is the word for it.'

'I have had fantasies along those lines, but I would be perfectly content to be merely in the same room as you, as we are now, only without these people around us.'

'So that you could hold my hand and tell me how lonely

you are, and that you are about to be sent off on a suicide mission, and that all you want before you go is the love of a good woman.'

'That's not my normal line of patter, but if it's a way to get to your heart, I'm prepared to try it.'

'You're sweet.'

She began pulling on her gloves.

'You're not going yet, are you?'

'I can't leave Jeremy with friends for long, it's a way of losing friends.'

'When can I see you again?'

'In synagogue every week. Why don't you come any more?'

'Can't, Saturday's my busiest day.'

'What are you, a Rabbi or something?'

'No, but you're getting warm. Can't we meet next week, same time, same place?'

'Same time, but not the same place.'

'Where then?'

She hesitated.

'At home.' And with that she was gone.

I had to sit down to take that in and, when I was given the bill, mathematician though I was, I got a different sum every time I totted up the figures. I felt shaky when I went out into the street. It all seemed too good to be true but I would have to wait a full week before I could establish whether this was not yet another daydream.

A little later I was standing at a tram-stop, still bathed in a glow of euphoria, when I was joined by a tall lean, dusky figure in the uniform of the Scots Guards, his features half-hidden by his cap visor. There was something vaguely familiar about him, and he must have found something vaguely familiar about me, but the person I thought he might be didn't quite go with the blue shoulder-flash of the Scots Guards, and he possibly felt that the person I was didn't quite go with the red shoulder-flash of the Polish army. Recognition descended on us in the same instant.

'Bernard!' I shouted.

'Sammy!' he cried.

But even as I spoke, the euphoria which had surrounded me vanished, and my surprise turned to envy.

What was my second or third cousin Bernard, alias Berale, Boyarski, who only came from Poland yesterday, doing in a crack regiment of the line, while I, Sammy the wonder boy, who was almost born in this country, was a sort of para-cleric in the Polish army, organizing prayers, distributing prayer-books and laying on *gefilte* fish for Friday-night suppers? I could have cried.

He asked me the inevitable questions about what I was doing in the Polish army and without telling him actual lies I must have given the impression that I was engaged in special duties (which of course I was) and he pressed me no further. He also wanted to know why, if I was stationed in Glasgow, I had not visited his family, which was slightly embarrassing, for we had more or less lost contact with them since the outbreak of war, and whether we had or hadn't, I was not in the least interested in resuming contact.

'I get very little time off,' I said.

'And when you do, you've got better things to do with it than visit relatives,' he said. 'I know what you mean. And in any case I'm not sure how you would be received. My parents are very upset with yours, at least my mother is.'

'But why?'

'Why do you think? Your sister's wedding.'

'But it was a tiny affair, we hardly invited anyone.'

'My mother, who has spies everywhere, said you even invited factory-hands from your father's work-place. Nothing that's happened in the war, not even the Clydeside blitz, upset her so much. She doesn't stop talking about it, and never will. She has a good memory for grievances. It was a relief to get into the army.'

We were both in a hurry and arranged to meet the following week, but the brief encounter told me a lot about myself, for it not only deprived me of my sense of euphoria, it left me steaming with chagrin. Gone was all thought of Emma, love, lust, and the only passion reigning in my breast was envy. I was determined, whatever else happened, to get out of the Polish army and into a fighting unit of the British army. I somehow felt that Mac would understand my feelings on the matter and as soon as I got back to barracks I marched unannounced into Holtzhacker's office and asked if he could arrange an appointment for me.

He blinked at me. 'Whatever for?'

'It's a private matter.'

'I'm here to deal with private matters.'

'It's not that sort of private matter.'

'Look, it's easier to see God than Mac these days. His adjutant will want to know why.'

'I want to leave the Polish army.'

'Don't we all?'

'I want a transfer to the British army.'

'Oh he won't take kindly to that, not Mac. He believes service in the Polish army is the greatest privilege to which a man can aspire. All the others are toy-soldiers, he'll tell you, the only fighting men in the allied forces are Poles.'

'But I don't happen to be a Pole.'

'Can I deal with it?'

'I'd rather handle it myself, if I may.'

The next morning, as if in answer to my anguish, a package arrived – by special messenger – with a travel pass, and orders signed by a Lt Col. Glover requiring me to report at an address in Aylesbury, Buckinghamshire at 1500 hours the following Wednesday, the very day, and almost the very hour, of my meeting with Emma.

I immediately phoned to tell her what had happened, and this time she answered (she was still in bed).

'I think it's all for the best, don't you?' she said.

'Perhaps.'

So much for my grand romance. It hadn't even occurred to me to put the date forward.

If all thought of Emma had been banished previously by envy, it was now suppressed by curiosity. I did not share father's feelings that the world owed me a commission, but I did think that my abilities, such as they were, could have been more fully used, and it now seemed that someone, somewhere, possibly even God in heaven, had reached the same conclusion, and the fact that the orders had arrived by special messenger suggested that my hour had finally come.

In Aylesbury I found myself in the cavernous hallway of what looked like a nunnery, which is indeed what it had been in an earlier incarnation. There was no Lt Col. Glover to greet me, but after a short wait I looked up to find a familiar figure standing over me. It was Dr MacFadyen, a former mathematics tutor at Manchester University.

'What the hell are you doing in the Polish army?' he said. I was by now a little tired of that question, but comforted myself with the assumption that I wouldn't be hearing it for much longer.

'Accident of fate,' I said.

'Like it?'

'There's a war on and one learns to take things as they come.'

'Well,' he said, 'you've got another thing coming.'

There was, he explained, a shortage of first-class mathematicians and he had been engaged to trawl them up wherever he could.

'I've rounded up every man, woman and child who's taken a first in the past fifty years, and they still want more. I don't know what they do with them all. I sometimes think they eat them, and for that matter I don't know what the hell they'll be doing with you. It's all so secret that I have not been trusted with the details, but you will report here in two weeks' time and you will be taken hence where you will receive further orders. I can also tell you that you will be out of uniform but subject to something more vigorous, in some ways, than military discipline, but you will have a status equivalent to that of a full lieutenant, with allowances, pay and conditions to match. You have a week to bid your fond farewells to the Polish army, and a further week's leave. May the Lord have mercy on your soul.'

And with that he vanished as suddenly as he appeared.

When I got back to Glasgow, my soul purged of envy, something of my tender feelings for Emma returned. They began to revive the minute I boarded the train and grew in force as I approached my destination. By the time I reached Glasgow they almost overwhelmed me. I jumped from the train as it was pulling into the platform and rushed for a telephone but, as fate would have it, her mother answered: 'Is that the corporal?'

'No, it's the lieutenant.'

'Which lieutenant?'

'The one who was the corporal.'

'She's not in.'

I scribbled a quick note suggesting a time and place for a meeting, and pushed it through her letter-box. The next morning I received a telegram: 'SORRY CANNOT MAKE IT STOP BEST OF LUCK IN NEW JOB STOP LOVE EMMA.'

I suppose I was expecting too much of fate, but I was reluctant to leave it at that. It occurred to me as I was travelling back in the train that it was rather presumptuous of a mere corporal to try and seduce the wife of a major, but now as a full lieutenant (even if pipless) I felt that I had a fuller claim to her favours and phoned her again, but her mother answered once more, and fearing yet another letter to Holtzhacker, I let the matter rest.

I had in recent weeks regarded Holtzhacker with growing distaste and had kept out of his way as far as I could, but now that I was about to see the last of him, something of my fondness for the old rascal returned and I broke my news to him with something like regret. He, for his part, charged me with ingratitude.

'Look at yourself, a corporal already. You could be a sergeant if you stayed on, and even as a corporal you were better off than half the officers.'

I felt tempted to remind him that I had never sought his favours, but was content instead to explain that I had no choice in the matter.

'I've still got a bit of influence you know, and could get Mac to put in a word for you.'

'It wouldn't help.'

'Mac? He can pick up the phone and speak to Churchill himself.'

'But I'm perfectly happy to move.'

'Have things been so hard for you here?'

'I need a change.'

'You'll get one.' He looked around him and lowered his voice. 'I shouldn't be telling you this, and you mustn't breathe a word to anyone, but we'll be landing in Europe any day now. We've only been playing games until now. In another few weeks things'll begin in earnest.'

'Too late, I'm afraid.'

'What exactly will you be doing?'

'Can't say.'

'Can't say because you don't know, or because you're not allowed to say?'

'Both.'

His eyes widened. 'You're not even born here and they trust you with real secrets?'

'Apparently.'

He rose to shake my hand and held on to it for an embarrassingly long time. 'I'll miss you,' he said. 'I may have bossed you around a bit, but that's a habit you get into the minute you get a pip on your shoulder, and even if I did, it's always been for your own good. I've looked upon you as a son from the day you came in your little short trousers and with your little thin pink knees, to teach me English. When I ran away from Manchester you were the only thing I missed. Very earnest little man you were, never smiled. I hope you'll find something to smile about now you're grown up. And I'll tell you something, if you don't find it in the army, you won't find it in civvy street. Now's your chance.'

He leaned forward and for a dreadful moment I thought he was going to kiss me, but he slapped my shoulder and said:

'I'll be hearing more of you, that I'm sure of, and I shouldn't be at all surprised if you'll hear more of me.'

He was to be proved right on both counts.

CHAPTER NINE

I hadn't realized how much my uniform meant to me until I surrendered it. It had given me, even as a man apart, a sense of belonging. I felt part of the crowd, one of the lads, or 'our lads' as we were referred to in the popular press. No matter how inert, lazy or useless one might be it marked one out as actively engaged in the war effort: it bestowed a warranty of official approval. Now, in mufti, I was again on my own and, though engaged in duties of 'the highest importance', I was looked at askance as a shirker or, worse, as a cripple. Moreover, as I now wore shoes instead of boots, I felt oddly shrunken.

Nor did I derive all that much joy from my new duties. MacFadyen's breathless whispers had led me to believe that I would be working in the innermost recesses of power, perhaps even in the Cabinet Office. I had to sign innumerable forms swearing me to secrecy and the work was indeed top secret. I had to give notice of my movements whenever I left town and I was cautioned to give no hint of the nature of my employment even to my closest relatives, but in fact I worked in the meteorological section of the Air Ministry, and not even as a weather-forecaster but, if I may coin an expression, as a rear-caster. Which is to say, I had to establish the incidence of weather patterns prevailing in different parts of Europe over the past twenty-five years, an activity so banal that I was grateful for the secrecy which surrounded it.

My colleagues were mostly college dons, many of them elderly, but several were contemporaries who, like me, were working in the Air Ministry as part of their national service.

There was little opportunity for social contact during working hours, for everyone beavered away in his own little cell, but we often came together for a drink in a local pub in the evening.

Going to a pub, by the middle of 1943, was a little like taking part in a lottery, for there wasn't always any certainty that they would have anything worth drinking at all. One asked for a whisky or a gin, but one often had to settle for a rum or a port or a sherry, or a benedictine, or an advocaat, or a green chartreuse, or a blue curaçao, or something which was a speciality of our local and which I called the black death, all of which made drinking a hazardous as well as a convivial activity, and added something to our sense of congeniality.

The head of our unit was a large, elderly, red-faced, one-armed Air Commodore, with a woebegone expression and sad, world-weary voice. He was not engaged in any of the technical work, but was in charge of the overall security and also acted in *loco parentis*, to see that none of us got out of hand, for we were an oddly assorted bunch, as mathematicians often are, only wartime conditions made us that much odder.

'You wouldn't believe what some of those chaps get up to in their cells,' he said.

He often presided at our gatherings in the pub, and the frequency with which he paid for the drinks made me suspect that he had a splash-fund to keep us happy.

Some of my colleagues were mathematicians of international rank, and they included Hugo Kleindorf, a tall, lean figure, with sunken cheeks, sunken chest and prematurely grey hair, who was something of a legend. Even as a sixth former in Manchester I had heard of him and was surprised to discover that he was only about six or seven years older then me. He was Austrian by birth and had come to work in Cambridge shortly before the war and, although he had fled from the Nazis, he was interned as an enemy alien in the Isle of Man in 1940, and it took the personal intervention of a Cabinet Minister to have him released and engaged in war work.

I wasn't certain of the exact nature of his work because, like the rest of us, he was not free to discuss it, but he was accorded the greatest deference by the Commodore who treated him like an anxious mother coping with a gifted but wayward child.

He himself believed that he was still under suspicion.

'I'm followed everywhere I go,' he said, 'and not very discreetly, which can be useful, for I often get lost, especially in the blackout, and I only have to turn to my shadow to be put right.'

He was animated in conversation and talked so rapidly as to be almost unintelligible, but in silent moments he looked unspeakably sad, and it was said that he was sighing for the loss of the Hapsburg Empire.

Most of us tended to be left-wingers, while he was fairly far to the right, which was possibly why he was still under suspicion. He was not an imperialist as such but believed that the dismemberment of the Hapsburg Empire had prepared the way for the rise of Hitler.

'There are too many small, warring nationalities in central and eastern Europe. They need someone to knock their heads together. Hitler's doing it for the moment. When he's gone, the Russians will take over. Empires are unavoidable.'

My new job, boring though it was, did have certain advantages. I was in London and for the first time in my life I was earning something like money, not a lot, but enough to enable me to rent a tiny attic flat at the top of a Georgian house in Bloomsbury. It was part of a terrace which had survived in a general area of desolation caused by the blitz, and it had about it the permanent smell of broken masonry, but I was in my own home.

I had spent a few days' leave in Manchester and had told father that I was to be a lieutenant, which I thought would please him, but he said:

'Lieutenant? Why only lieutenant? Young Krieger's a captain.'

'For goodness sake,' said mother. 'He's hardly been a year in the army, what do you expect him to be, a general?'

I did not, at that point, have the heart to tell them that they would never see any external signs of my new status. They both seemed to have aged considerably in the five or six months since I was last home. Father, who was about fifty (I was never too sure about the age of either of them), had been grey haired at forty, but he was now grey faced and grey voiced and did not seem to have the same robustness of voice or build, while mother seemed almost decrepit.

The tide of war had turned and the allies were advancing in almost every direction, but things were becoming increasingly difficult on the home front. One hardly lived off the fat of the land in the army, but one was insulated from actual shortages. It was otherwise at home. One's rations assured the bare minimum. Everything else involved long queues. Fish involved one wait, bread another, fruit and vegetables a third, and as there was rarely any certainty of getting, say, potatoes, onions and sprouts in one shop, mother sometimes had to queue in two or three.

'There's only the two of us at home and I eat in the works canteen,' said father, 'I don't know why she needs to do all that shopping.' Neither did I, until I discovered that she also shopped around for a house-bound elderly neighbour. I suggested that it was about time she showed a little concern for herself.

'I like to get out and about,' she said. 'You meet interesting people in queues,' and she made it seem as if shopping was not so much a dreary chore as a social excursion, but she did look worn out and was often breathless and wheezy.

If I worried about my parents I had the feeling that they were getting to be a trifle worried about me.

'What sort of people will you be meeting in your new job?' father asked, 'you're not getting any younger, you know,' by which he of course meant, 'What are your chances of meeting a nice Jewish girl?'

I did, in fact, meet a girl called Sarah, who with her dark hair, dark eyes and sallow complexion, looked vaguely Jewish but who, as I discovered later, was Anglican, but it was not the sort of subject which featured a great deal in our conversation. She was a nicely formed girl and would have been handsome had she paid more attention to her appearance. Clothes-rationing did not leave much scope for elegance, but the other girls in the building still managed to look fairly smart, whereas she displayed a dowdiness which seemed not so much accidental, as contrived. She normally wore glasses and the one concession she made to vanity was in removing them the moment she left the office, though I in fact thought she suited them, for they made her eyes look larger and more lustrous. She had the deep, rapid voice of a public-school girl, though she told me that her father was a railwayman, which was true and it was only later that I discovered he was a director of the the London and North Eastern Railway. She was down from Cambridge and was Kleindorf's secretary.

We went out to concerts together and sometimes dined in Soho, but she always insisted on paying her share.

'I happen to know exactly what you're earning,' she said, 'and unless you have private means, you can't really afford to take me out this often.'

There were two drawbacks to our relationship. She lived in south London and anything south of the river was a wilderness to me. I had what I liked to think of as a chivalrous streak which was not unmixed with a lecherous one. I felt obliged to see her home through the blackout after a night out, but hoped that once I had done so I would be rewarded with more than a cup of coffee, but she was always afraid I would miss the last tram – something I was prepared to hazard – and rarely gave me a chance even to take my coat off.

The second drawback was rather more serious: she was said to be Kleindorf's mistress. Moral attitudes became fairly relaxed in wartime and there were rumours that almost every woman in the building, and not a few of the men, was somebody's mistress, and that everybody was sleeping with everybody else. I, however, suspected that the rumours about Kleindorf and Sarah were probably true.

She sometimes joined us for drinks in the pub after work, which I thought was rather daring, for it was unusual in those days for respectable young women to be seen drinking in a public bar, and I'm not at all sure that I approved, especially as I had the feeling that, though her and Kleindorf's eyes rarely met, there were unseen signals passing between them, and, indeed, the very fact that their eyes didn't meet almost confirmed my suspicions.

I could, of course, have asked her straight out about Kleindorf, but it would have been presumptuous to do so, for our relationship had not gone far enough for that. Our conversation, when we were out together, was mainly about books we had read, pictures we had seen, places we had been to (she was fairly widely travelled), and people we knew. Unlike my encounter with Emma, our meetings were strangely devoid of anything erotic, or even suggestive. She was far more educated and intelligent than Emma and had more to say for herself, but although we held hands occasionally, and rubbed noses, and even kissed, I was not roused by her as I had been by Emma or Theresa, but then Theresa and Emma were forbidden fruit, which she was not.

Then one day, rather unexpectedly, I received a letter from my sister, 'Haven't seen you for ages,' she wrote. 'Father tells me you have a VERY senior job, doing VERY secret work. You MUST come and tell me all about it. Bring a friend (a girlfriend, that is) if you have one.'

That last line was more of a challenge than an invitation, and almost on impulse I asked Sarah if she would like to spend a weekend with me at my sister's and, a little to my surprise, perhaps even dismay, she accepted.

Knowing my sister, I should have asked what sort of arrangements she had in mind for us and I took it (as I presumed did Sarah) that we would each have our own room, but I began to have doubts on the matter during the train journey, and by the time we reached our destination I must have looked fairly distraught, for the first thing Sosh said to me when she opened the door was: 'Are you all right? Did the journey not agree with you?' Sarah, for her part, was completely at ease, and when I mumbled an introduction, Sosh gave me a look which said, or seemed to say, 'You've done better for yourself than I imagined.' They chatted away merrily over tea while I, unable to eat or drink, waited impatiently to see what was in store upstairs. Finally, after what seemed an eternity, Sosh said: 'I'd better show you to your room.'

Sarah gave me a look which seemed more inquiring than troubled, which eased my feelings a little, and I bolted down a sandwich which had remained untouched on my plate.

The house was a red-brick terrace, tall and narrow, so that one could hardly move without going up or down. Our room was on the very top floor and the breathlessness I felt was not entirely due to the climb.

Sosh led the way, telling us something of the history of the place as she went. 'It belongs to the church and was used mainly by clergymen,' she said, 'and it still smells a bit of bibles and books, but don't let that put you off.'

She opened the door of a small room which was largely taken up by a huge canopied bed, showed us the adjoining bathroom, gave me a broad wink, and was gone.

Sarah looked at me with a grin.

'What's amusing you?' I said.

'You're embarrassed, aren't you?'

'Who said so?'

'You look it. Would you rather we had separate rooms?'

'No, no, my goodness, no.'

'You're quite sure?'

'Of course.'

'Then kiss me, at least, seeing we're alone together.'

We were standing against the bed and as we kissed she fell back on to it, with me on top, and I began to grope under her dress.

'Save it,' she said. 'I want a bath first.'

She seemed to be an uncommonly long time in the bath. I looked around the room. I gazed out of the window. I examined the prints of Biblical scenes on the landing. When I tired of that, I began to descend the stairs, but hesitated. I had no wish to enter into conversation with my sister at that particular moment and finally, for want of anything better to do, I sat down on the edge of the bed and began reading, but my mind was on other things, or, in particular, on another thing.

When she finally emerged with a towel round her body and another round her head, I stood there open mouthed. She was still moist and steaming, as I was in a moment, and that without the benefit of a bath.

'Would you like to dry me,' she said. 'I like being rubbed up the wrong way.'

I pulled off her towel and she stood there like a bashful Venus with one hand over her bosom and the other over her pubic hair. I had never in my twenty-two years of life seen a live, fully grown, naked woman. It really was a wondrous sight.

'Well,' she said, 'what are you waiting for?'

I took the towel in both hands and begun rubbing her frantically.

'That's enough,' she said, and as she put her arms round me we sank on to the bed.

I kissed her on her mouth, her neck, her breasts, her navel.

'Go on,' she whispered, 'for God's sake don't stop.'

I began to tremble.

'Save it,' she said, 'save it, don't shoot your bolt yet.' And she rose and undressed me before climbing on top of me.

When it was over, we both began shivering and dived under the blankets.

'You're a bit slow, aren't you?' she said.

'In which way?'

'Why didn't you come into the bath? The door wasn't locked, and I was there long enough. You might at least have offered to scrub my back.'

'Did you expect me to?'

'That's what I mean by being slow. And another thing. You've got a flat in London, haven't you? Why did you never invite me back? Why did you have to wait till we stayed with your sister before getting into bed with me?'

That, indeed, was the very question I had been asking myself while she was still in the bath.

'I was beginning to wonder if you were a pansy,' she said.

I laughed at that. 'You're beginning to sound like my sister.'

'Does she think you're a pansy?'

'She had fears along those lines.'

'Is that why you brought me here, to reassure her? You can tell her you did very well – for a beginner.'

'What makes you think I'm a beginner?'

'Your awkwardness, your impatience – you don't really know your way around. I should imagine that if you've had any previous experience at all it was something fumbled and unexpected.'

'Unexpected, yes. Fumbled, no.'

'Probably with a woman your mother's age.'

'Older.'

'Tell me about her.'

'An enigmatic woman. Rather grand, very beautiful, somewhat tragic.'

'And you fell hopelessly in love with her.'

'As a matter of fact I did, though there was a time when I thought I was in love with her daughter.'

'Because she was an accessible version of her mother.'

'She wasn't all that accessible, at least not to me, but you could be right. How come you're so experienced?'

'The school I went to was next door to a military academy; the University I went to had twenty men to every woman, and the ratio in my present job is about the same.'

'Have they been grand passions or casual one-night stands?'

'Grand passions, though some have been grander than others.'

I was trying to lead on to Kleindorf, but our conversation was interrupted by a knock on the door and Sunny's voice calling: 'Come and get it!'

I had a quick shower while she dressed, but when I emerged she pulled the towel from me and we began all over again.

Sosh seemed a trifle put out when we came downstairs.

'You may find the food a bit overdone,' she said testily, but Sunny was all smiles and insisted over her protests that we have drinks first, which was just as well, for I had need of a stiff whisky.

American servicemen – or at least American officers – seemed hardly touched by the war, for we were treated to a quality of food and a quantity of liquor the like of which I had not known since that memorable evening when I treated Sosh to a meal in the Midland Hotel.

We talked about the war and Sunny said it was all over bar the shouting.

'I take it you'll be moving to New York,' I said, at which he exchanged looks with Sosh.

'That's a war I shall have to fight when the war's over,' he said, 'but you can take it that I won't.'

'You can take it that I will,' said Sosh.

'I've fallen in love with England,' he said. 'Salisbury, the cathedrals, Winchester, Bath, Hereford, Wells, Worcester, I don't think I could live anywhere else.'

'I've met cricket bores, and football bores and rugby

bores,' said Sosh, 'but there's no bore like a cathedral bore. Ever since we moved to Salisbury he's spent more time in the cathedral than with me.'

'Wait till you get to Italy,' said Sarah.

'I've been to Italy,' said Sunny, 'but I found St Peter's, St Mark's and the rest too gaudy and grand, like the set of a Cecil B. de Mille epic.'

'He doesn't sound very American, does he?' said Sosh.

Sunny had to rush back to his base shortly after dinner and Sosh and Sarah washed up in the kitchen while I cleared up in the dining room. They were chatting and laughing away together like lifelong friends and on the few occasions I intruded upon them, their conversation suddenly stopped, either because they were talking about me, or because they were touching upon matters too indelicate for my innocent ears.

When they finished, Sarah went upstairs. I was still busy Hoovering the dining-room carpet when Sosh came in and told me to stop.

'There are still some crumbs there – '

'They can stay there till tomorrow.'

'They'll be trodden in.'

'Since when have you been so house-proud?'

'I've always been tidy, you know that.'

'You're afraid to talk to me, aren't you?'

'What makes you say that?'

'Because you've been avoiding my eyes all evening. I was young myself once, you know, and was not in the least scandalized by what was going on upstairs, only I thought you took your time over it. Even so, I was thrilled to bits at the thought of my bookish little brother having a bit of fun at last. And I like her, though she's not at all what I expected.'

'What did you expect?'

'Someone nice and kosher, a nice Jewish girl from a nice Jewish home.'

'Would a nice Jewish girl from a nice Jewish home have come away for a dirty weekend?'

'You'd be surprised what nice Jewish girls can get up to – after all, I was supposed to have been one myself. In any case, we have two spare bedrooms, so the weekend needn't have been dirty.'

'So why did you put us in one?'

'Because it was jolly well about time that you did have a dirty weekend. Good God, if you don't have one in wartime when will you? I was taking a risk, of course, but I'm glad to see it paid off. Was this the first time you were – how shall I put it? – together?'

'There are some questions which even a sister shouldn't ask.'

'How long have you been going out?'

'Two or three months, not on any regular basis, but I see her most weekends.'

'So this wasn't the first time?'

'Will you mind your own bloody business.'

'Sorry, I seem to be touching on a sore point – or is that an indelicate way of putting it?'

'Sosh, I think you sometimes go out of your way to embarrass me.'

'Are you serious about her?'

'Why do you ask?'

'Because I think she's serious about you.'

'I doubt it, because I have reason to believe there's another.'

'Then why did she come away with you?'

'Because he's not generally available at weekends.'

'Ah, I get it. You're her Sunny.'

'Sort of.'

'Then why don't you ask her straight out?'

'Did Sunny ever ask you straight out?'

'He had no idea that Safran even existed. Not that it would have made any difference. He would have clung on to me in any circumstances. In any case, I was only twenty. She must be thirty.'

'She's nowhere near thirty.'

'She can't be far short of it. Not that it's important, you've always been old for your age. I'm sure she'd like to marry and settle down and start a family. She'd have you like a shot. You'd be doing well for yourself. She's lively, intelligent, attractive, and I have the feeling that she's got money behind her.'

'What has that to do with it?'

'Because you've got none behind you. What can you do with a maths degree? Teach in school? University? How much does even a Professor earn?'

'Enough to meet my needs.'

'But not hers. Have you looked at her clothes, her shoes? They may not be very stylish, but the sort of English frumpishness she goes in for costs money and lots of it. She would make a good University wife. I can't see father being too happy about it, or mother, but what's more to the point, would you be all that happy? I know you're no longer Holtzhacker's altar-boy, and that you no longer rush to synagogue every time you have a free minute, but you've still got an indelible kosher streak. I noticed it after dinner when you wouldn't have milk in your coffee.'

'I could forgo milk, but I doubt if I would have been able to resist the temptation of cream. What you're trying to tell me is that you can't see me marrying out of the faith. You may be right, but our relationship hasn't got that far, and may not get that far.'

'It will, I think it already has. We established a rapport almost from the moment she stepped over the threshold, and we talked together like sisters. She, of course, wanted to know all about you.'

'And so, of course, you told her.'

'Why not? Though she told me a few things about you which I didn't know. Who was the grand dame?'

'What grand dame?'

'The great love of your life.'

'Frankly, it's none of your business.'

'Of course it isn't, but I'm dying to know. Was it Sue's mother?'

'Sue? Sue who?'

'Sue Mulloy, remember, the dark little thing, Pippa's cousin. All her friends went for her mother, but I wouldn't have thought she was your type, or you hers. Pippa's mother would have been more up your street, but she's not very accessible. Safran was besotted with her as a schoolboy, you know, the great love of his life. He thought I looked rather like her. Wish I did.'

I thought I had purged Theresa from my soul, but I found

the sound of his name linked with hers painful, possibly because I had an uneasy feeling that he may have been granted the same privileges as me.

I had, even with all the whisky which Sunny kept pouring into my glass, not been entirely at ease over dinner, but I did derive immense reassurance from the sight of Sunny and Sosh together. When I was at their wedding I thought that the whole thing was doomed and that she was only going through the ceremony because she had been overwhelmed by a passing sense of guilt induced by father's illness, and that she would resume her liaison with Safran the moment she was back to her more usual self, but I was clearly mistaken, for I felt that I was in the presence of a thoroughly happy couple. There was no sort of lovey-dovey nonsense between them, and my suspicions would have been immediately aroused if there had been, but though they rarely touched, and sometimes argued, the affection between them was almost palpable. Now, the very sound of his name brought the doubts flooding back.

'Are you still seeing him?'

'Safran? What a question to ask. I'm a respectable married woman,' which was not quite the categorical assurance I had hoped for.

'He's in India, in case you're interested,' she added, which did not reassure me either, for it suggested they were still in touch.

When I got upstairs Sarah had changed into a silk dressing-gown and was sitting in front of the mirror brushing her hair which fell in regular waves down to her shoulders. I liked her with her hair down and kissed her on the neck.

'You were a long time,' she said,

'I haven't seen my sister since her wedding, so we had a lot to talk about.'

'I like your sister, she's lively and attractive –'

'Those are almost the very words she used about you.'

'Did she? I hope she meant it, because I felt I was being weighed and measured.'

'The one good thing about my sister is that you know exactly where you are with her. If she didn't like you, you'd have known it from the moment you entered.'

'She didn't like the things I wore, I can tell you that much. She's a bit of a clothes-horse, isn't she? I don't know any other woman who dresses so well in war time.'

'She has an American husband and can order clothes from American mail-order catalogues, and before she got married she used to steal my clothing-coupons, and mother's and father's. I was under the impression that you had established an immediate rapport.'

'We did once the drinks started flowing, but now that they have worn off, I'm beginning to feel slightly resentful. I don't really know why, I suppose it may be because I gave away too much of myself. I noticed that she didn't drink nearly as much as I did.'

'She never does, but then Sosh sober is less inhibited than most people drunk.'

'Did you ask her to put us together in one room, or was that her idea?'

'Hers.'

'I thought as much. Rather presumptuous don't you think? I'm sure she would have found me a separate room if I'd asked for it, but it would have been embarrassing. I don't like making a demonstration of my innocence. On the other hand I don't like my lack of innocence being taken for granted. She obviously thinks I've been around.'

'She thinks everyone's been around, but then she's been around herself. I wouldn't worry about it.'

I leaned over her shoulder and slid my hands down the inside of her nightgown. Her breasts swelled at my touch.

At that moment the phone went. I stiffened. Phone calls at that time of the night, like telegrams at almost any time, were bad news. A little later Sosh came to the door.

'That was father,' she said. 'Alfred's dead.'

'Alfred? Alfred who?'

'How many Alfreds do you know? Theresa's husband, Pippa's father. Poor sod, forgotten already in his own lifetime.'

CHAPTER TEN

Father, as the former Life President of a synagogue, was an old hand at funerals, and used to spend most of his Sundays at one burial ground or another. He had also attended the funerals of workmates who had died in the blitz, but this was rather different. It was a cremation, and he dressed for it as he might have dressed for a wedding. In his Life President's regalia of black jacket and striped trousers, but a bowler hat instead of a topper. Mother came in a black Persian lamb coat she had not worn since the outbreak of war. I arrived in the brown suit I was wearing. It was dark brown, but not dark enough for father, and if he had had the clothing-coupons to spare, he would have brought me a black suit there and then.

We were the first ones there and looked round uneasily at the unfamiliar surroundings, the banks of flowers, the polished pews, the stained-glass windows. From somewhere up high there came the sombre strains of organ music.

'You sure this isn't a church?' said father.

A little later we were joined by a pampered-looking pair in well-tailored outfits. They nodded politely to us, and we nodded back, but they kept their distance, and we kept ours. Other strangers began to drift in in ones and twos and settled in the pews. Most sat in silence, but here and there stray tributes floated on the chilly air. 'Fine fellow ... Poor fellow ... One of the best ... Straight as a die ... A gentleman ...'

The chapel gradually filled up. I recognized one or two faces I had seen at Pippa's ball, including Sue Mulloy, her little white face half-hidden in a fluffy fur collar. I nodded to her, and she nodded back, a trifle hesitantly, I thought, as if she didn't quite recognize me.

'Who's that?' said father, no doubt surprised that I should

have any acquaintances at all in such exalted surroundings.

'A niece,' I said.

'Rodger's niece?'

'Yes.'

'Good-looking girl.'

The funeral party arrived. Theresa looked stunning in a black fur coat, black hat with a short black veil, and black suede boots, Pippa, beside her, likewise in black, looked mousy in comparison, and washed out. Behind them came Edwin with a blonde, pink-cheeked young woman, pretty as a doll and as painted.

'Married six weeks ago,' father whispered. 'We get invited to the funerals, but not the weddings.'

The organ played an extract from a Handel oratorio. A Rabbi read two Psalms. A tall, distinguished-looking man whose swarthy features seemed vaguely familiar, read out a brief tribute, and finished, rather unexpectedly, with some lines from Shakespeare in a voice which suggested that if he was not an actor, he harboured ambitions to be one:

His life was gentle, and the elements
So mixed in him that Nature might stand up
And say to all the world, 'This was a Man!'

The Rabbi read a third Psalm, the organ ceased, a small pair of curtains in the wall opened, the coffin, which had been obscured by the banks of flowers, began to move till it vanished from view; the curtains closed. Curtains! It was as quick as that.

This was my first experience of a cremation and I decided there and then that whatever direction my faith (or lack of it) might take, I would insist on a good, old-fashioned kosher burial under six feet of earth. A cremation was too final and abrupt. I never believed in resurrection, but there was no harm in having one's bones in order just in case. It also seemed rather spiteful and wasteful. It was almost like saying, if I can no longer have any benefit from my body, nobody else will. I felt that the least one could do after a lifetime on earth was to pay for one's tenure by leaving something – almost like a tip under a plate – for the worms.

Sosh had been surprised when I began packing the minute

she gave me the message. 'Did old Rodgers mean all that much to you?' she said.

'In an odd way, he did.'

'He wouldn't have travelled across England to get to your funeral,' she said, and I suspect she thought I was using his death as an excuse to get away from Sarah. Sarah may even have felt the same, for she looked highly sceptical when I explained that he was a very old and dear friend who had brought us all over from Poland and had helped to establish my father in business, and the more I went into details the more sceptical she looked, and she finally said: 'You'd better go or you'll miss your train.'

The journey took me eighteen hours in all so I had ample time to examine my motives.

I began packing almost as a reflex action, but I did have genuine feelings about Rodgers. I liked his affable personality, his diffident manner, his tentative smile.

Diffidence was not an unknown quality in the circles in which I moved, but it was rarely combined with wealth, or even solvency. As soon as a man like my father, or Krieger, made a pound more than his neighbour, he began to throw his weight about and felt entitled to a place at the right hand of God, yet here was a man who with all his wealth and influence somehow still managed to seem shy and retiring. Perhaps he was too diffident for his own good, for in the end he lost his money, but he represented my first encounter with a gentleman. He also, I was frequently told, followed my progress with great interest and although I saw him rarely, the thought of his interest was a little like having fate smiling fondly upon me. Unfortunately, by the time I had grown to maturity, fate had ceased to smile fondly upon him, and yet instead of helping him in his débâcle, I added to it by sleeping with his wife. He, of course, knew nothing about it and, given the state of his mind, it is unlikely that he would have cared, but that, if anything, aggravated the offence, and it seemed to me that my main motive for rushing through the night to his funeral was by way of atonement. Yet once I was there I was no longer so sure, for I could hardly take my eyes off his widow.

After the service she and her children stood by the door to

shake hands or exchange kisses with the mourners as they filed out. I for some reason was among the last to leave, and was uncertain whether to offer my hand or my cheek. She also hesitated, but then as I moved forward to kiss her cheek, our lips met, which left me shaken.

'You're coming back with us aren't you?' she said. 'I'd like a word with you.'

She didn't say back where and I thought she may have meant Buxton, but a shortish, well-groomed man with red cheeks and wavy grey hair, came up to my parents and me and introduced himself as Mr Naseby. 'Edwin's father-in-law,' he added with more than a touch of pride in his voice. 'I have some taxis waiting, perhaps you'd like to come back with us.'

We were driven to a large red-brick house in south Manchester with expensive drapes, thick carpets and crystal chandeliers.

'A bankrupt rag-merchant,' father whispered. 'I should do so well with my prosperity as he does with his bankruptcy.'

One woman took our coats and a further two were serving tea. I was looking around for Theresa when I felt a tap on my shoulders and I turned to find myself face to face with a small, intense-looking girl with large eyes.

'Remember me?' she said.

'Yes,' I said, 'you're Sue Mulloy.'

'You were looking at me rather blankly in the crematorium, as if you didn't know who I was.'

'It's five years since we last met – '

'And I've changed out of all recognition.'

'You haven't actually – '

'I jolly well have, or at least I hope I have. I was an odious little brat. I shudder whenever I think of the person I was. You've changed a good deal, I can tell you. You looked like a well-scrubbed schoolboy in a fancy suit.'

'And now.'

'You don't look all that well scrubbed.'

'I don't feel it either. I've been travelling for nearly two days.'

'Just to get to the funeral? That's sporting of you. There are people who wouldn't cross the road to get there. Mother wasn't there, you know. Mind you, she had a reason for it. She thinks Aunt Theresa killed him, though it was a mercy if she did. Edwin got married about six weeks ago, a tiny affair, immediate family only. She wheeled him in to witness the ceremony, and he just sat there with hunched shoulders and his little fixed, lop-sided grin, not taking in a thing. I cried all night. That's why there were so few tears at the funeral, we mourned for him while he was still alive. He was the dearest, sweetest, kindest man I knew.'

She began crying. I nearly broke down myself at that moment. I pulled out my handkerchief and she grabbed it and rushed to another room. I followed.

'Leave me,' she sobbed. 'I'm unsightly when I'm in tears. My eyes get red and swollen and my face gets blotchy. I think I'm the only person who really cared for him. Everybody else was interested in him only when he was rich. The moment he lost his money they forgot he ever lived.'

'There was a fairly decent turn-out at the funeral.'

'Not compared to the sort of turn-outs at his dinners and balls. Hardly any of the people he used to hob-nob with in his prime, his grand friends, the Safrans, the Clairmans and others, turned up.'

'So who are all these people next door?'

'Mostly Edwin's in-laws, or people like your parents, Jewish Jews, the sort my mother dismisses as vulgar, pushy and uncouth, but they do at least take funerals seriously.'

She was able to solve one small mystery for me. When Edwin was at Sosh's wedding he had introduced us to a dark-haired young girl as his fiancée, whereas his wife was not only blonde, but her very features looked different.

'It's the same girl,' she said, 'but her mother runs a beauty parlour while her father has a dress-shop, so she assumes a new persona every week.'

She went upstairs to give herself a 'face-lift', as she called it, and I went back into the drawing room. Theresa appeared at that moment, looking almost slight without her fur coat and hat. Her hair, which used to stand up in waves, was now severely pulled back with a mid-parting and it somehow gave her eyes a searching quality.

'I'm so glad you were able to come,' she said. 'Alfred's

memory was almost gone by the time he died, poor man, but he had lucid moments and mentioned your name with surprising frequency. Only last week we were going over some family photos and there were several of the ball we gave for Pippa just before the war – five years almost to the day. Different world, wasn't it? He had more than an inkling it was nearly over. Anyway there was this rather lovely photo of you and Sue, and he said, "That's young Hoch, isn't it? Whatever happened to him?" You meant a lot to him, and I thought you might like to have one or two of his things as keepsakes. I'd like to put the place in order first, but if you should be home after the summer perhaps you could come over and see what you'd like to choose.'

I was deeply touched by the idea, until Pippa repeated the offer in less sentimental terms. She had a month's leave, she told me, and she was going to spend it in making their home habitable.

'Father could never bring himself to part with anything and the place is a like a junk-shop. If you should ever be in need of cuff-links, tie-pins, collar-studs, trouser-presses, shoehorns, corkscrews, hairbrushes, shaving-kits, hair-nets, paper-weights, cigarette-lighters, cigar-circumcisers, eyeshades, hip-flasks, tropical helmets, bowler-hats, panama hats, straw boaters, walking-sticks, shooting-sticks or snowshoes, come round and help yourself, but bring a wheelbarrow.'

I asked if her mother would remain in Buxton.

'Why not?'

'All by herself?'

'By herself? Mother? She wasn't by herself while father was alive, and she won't be by herself now he's dead. You need shed no tears for mother. I've been trying to persuade her to convert the house into a high-class brothel – Buxton could do with one – but she thought the suggestion in bad taste.'

I asked her about her own plans.

'I've none,' she said. 'All I want to do is to get as far away from here and from everyone I know as possible.'

My parents tried to persuade me to stay the night, but I had to be back in London in the morning and I took an evening train which, because of damage on the line, turned out to be a night train and I arrived at the office red-eyed, crumpled, unshaven and unwashed.

When I got to my cell, a messenger was waiting for me with a caseful of papers, but when I reached for my keyring to open it, it wasn't there. I searched frantically about my person, my coat, my jacket, my waistcoat, my trousers. I went through every article in my case, and then through my pockets again, with the messenger at my side, his grin getting wider and wider. I might have left it either at my sister's or in Manchester or, worse still, on the train. The Commodore had a duplicate, but to lose, or mislay, a key in a job like mine was every bit as serious as losing a rifle.

I asked the messenger to leave the case and come back later.

'That's against regulations,' he said with a malignant glint in his eyes.

I phoned the Commodore, who expressed no surprise and asked for no explanations, but came over, unlocked the case, and left without saying a word. I had no doubt that I would be hearing from him later.

At lunch-time he took me out for a drink.

'Sarah tells me you've had a bereavement. Someone close?'

'Very.'

'Sorry to hear it. Why didn't you ask for leave? I daresay hard work is the best way of getting over these things, but, if I may say so, you do look a bit the worst for wear. Why not take a couple of days off?'

'You've seen the case-load of papers.'

'They can wait. Have a drink, go to bed, that's my advice.'

It was more than advice. Coming from the Commodore – though paternally put – it was an order. I phoned Sarah, but she was out of the office, and I picked up my coat and case and went home, and then found that I had not only lost my office keys, but my house key and I had to seek out my landlord before I could get into my own flat.

I had left in a great hurry on Friday and the bed was unmade, the floor was unswept and the sink was piled high with an accumulation of unwashed cutlery and crockery, and the place reminded me a little of poor Alfred's home during that memorable visit to Buxton and, although it was already June, it felt more like January. I was too tired to light a fire and the one-bar electric radiator offered hardly any heat. I was normally tidy, even house-proud, but my weariness – I had not slept for three nights – got the better of me, and so I had a bath and went to bed.

Towards evening there was a ring at the door. I put on my dressing-gown and went downstairs to answer. It was Sarah.

'I hear you've been poorly,' she said.

'A bit travel-stained,' I said. We kissed, and I led the way upstairs.

'You'll have to excuse the mess,' I said. 'I wasn't expecting company.'

'I'll bet my mess is bigger than yours,' she said, but when she entered the flat and looked around her she agreed that I had the edge on her.

'It's not usually like this,' I said.

'Let me give you a hand to clear it up a bit,' and before I could stop her, she grabbed an apron, rolled up her sleeves and was in the kitchen washing the dishes, and watching her I could almost see Theresa.

'This has been a revelation,' she said. 'Everything about you, your office, your reports, the way you dress, even your conversation, is so tidy, that when you apologized for the mess, I thought you might be harbouring a speck of dust on your mantelpiece, but this is the real thing.'

While she was busy in the kitchen and living room, I went into the bedroom, made the bed, tidied up the room, washed, shaved and changed into my suit. I had always thought of myself as self-sufficient, but I liked the idea of having a woman around the house.

When I emerged, I hardly recognized the place: I hadn't seen it in such order since the day I moved in.

'My God, you are good – and so quick! No wonder the Commodore swears by you.'

'The Commodore swears by everybody. He's very proud of his unit and claims he has more geniuses per square foot than any other establishment in the country. He was very upset when you turned up without your keys this morning.'

'That's supposed to be a secret.'

'There are no secrets from me. Blotted your copy-book, haven't you? But I shouldn't worry too much. Everyone's entitled to at least one blot, and the fact that you've had none almost placed you under suspicion. Kleindorf loses everything he's ever given. He's no longer trusted with keys.'

'Yes, but Kleindorf's Kleindorf.'

'Kleindorf was Kleindorf.'

'What do you mean?'

'He's vanished. People do all the time, as you know, but he vanished so suddenly and completely that even I didn't know anything about it. He wasn't in his office this morning, but then he's never been particularly regular in his comings and goings, then shortly before I left, the Commodore put his head round the door and said he wouldn't be back.'

This was momentous news, and I was surprised at the casual way in which she had let it slip, as if to suggest that there was nothing special between them, but perhaps there *was* nothing between them.

'Weren't you upset?'

'I was a bit. I know he couldn't talk about his work, and one is shifted around at very short notice, but he was in the office on Friday morning and I thought he might have given some hint, but there we are. I spent the last half hour before I left, clearing out his desk. You wouldn't believe what I found there. Moulding sandwiches, a half-eaten sausage, fountain-pens which had been borrowed from everybody in the building, but never returned, a Gideon Bible, and a very substantial collection of filthy pictures, the sort of thing my brothers brought back from Port Said. Odd chap.'

'Weren't you two – ?'

'Lovers? Hardly. I met him at Cambridge. He arrived with an international reputation, and I fell for his reputation, but there was something about his lean and hungry look which I found appealing. He was married already then, to a woman ten years older than him, a devout Catholic like an overweight madonna, with a cross in her cleavage large enough to crucify a man. She remained in Cambridge, and he saw her at weekends. I kept him company during the week, on and off. I suppose at the back of my mind was the feeling he might leave her, because for the life of me I don't know what he gets out of his marriage. She hasn't got looks or intelligence. You might think, given her bulk, she might at least have warmth, but she hasn't even that. She's a large, rather stupid, peasant woman and I suppose it's like having a piece of mother earth.'

'Is it all over now?'

'I thought it was all over years ago, but then he phoned out of the blue and asked if I wanted to be his secretary, and I dropped everything I was doing and down I came.'

'Supposing he was to phone you again?'

'I'm that much older and wiser, and so is he. I honestly don't think he would. Aren't you going to offer me a cup of tea?'

I did better than that. There was little in the house in the way of food, but I took the few rotting potatoes, onions and carrots I found about the place, with a half-eaten leg of chicken, and made a reasonable soup out of them. I then opened a tin of spam, which we ate with wine and we both felt pleased with our repast.

'It doesn't quite compare with your sister's cuisine,' she said, 'but I shall recommend it to all my friends.'

As we were clearing up I took her by the waist and began nibbling her ear.

'Not now,' she said. 'I feel a bit grubby. I must have a bath first.'

'I had a bath only a few hours ago, the water won't be hot.'

'I don't mind a cold bath.'

In the event it was lukewarm, but I joined her. It is difficult to feel romantic, or even erotic, when one is covered in goose-pimples and it was not until we got into bed that we recovered sufficient bodily warmth to make love.

Bright sunshine streamed through a gap in the curtains when we woke the next morning, as if the endless winter had been finally sloughed off, and it not only filled my room, it seemed to fill my very soul. There was something quite heavenly in going to bed with an attractive young woman and waking up on a sunny morning to find her by one's side.

I leaned over to kiss her.

'Not now,' she said. 'Not before I've brushed my teeth and had a bath.'

'Another bath? You must live in water.'

'I do. When I was at college they used to call me the amphibian.'

'I shan't get in with you, or we'll be late for work.'

'What work? The Commodore said you were having a couple of days off, and I've no work to go to. No doubt they'll fix me up with something eventually, but in the meantime I'm virtually unemployed.'

And so we bathed together, and then over breakfast I suggested that she move in with me.

'I would, but for two things. I don't know if you'll have enough hot water for the two of us – '

'I'll boil water up in a kettle, if necessary.'

'And then there's my piano. I used to fancy myself as something of a pianist before the war, and I still like to practise every day if I can.'

'I'll get you a piano.'

'You've no room for it.'

'I'll throw my bed out to make room, but you shall have a piano,' and she agreed to bring some of her things over that evening.

'There's no point in bringing everything over,' she said. 'I don't know what sort of plans the Commodore may have for me. I could be posted to Calcutta.'

There was hardly any food in the house and she kindly offered to help me with my shopping, but when we emerged into the street we were immediately aware of a sense of excitement in the air, and I wasn't sure whether something momentous had happened in the world about us, whether it was induced by our happiness, or whether it was simply brought on by the sudden emergence of the sun. When we turned the corner we found the answer. Special editions of the morning papers had been rushed out to announce that the allies had landed in Normandy. It was D-Day.

I was, of course, delighted with the news, yet regarded it with something like chagrin. Why could it not have come a week earlier? Our private elation had been upstaged by a public event, and it was some time before we could turn our thoughts to our personal affairs.

The allies were slow to break out of their beachheads, but the Russians were advancing rapidly on the Eastern Front, and it seemed likely that the war would be finished by Christmas. Sarah asked me what I would do when it was all over.

'I haven't given much thought to it, but I have toyed with the idea of going on to Cambridge for another degree, or looking round the Universities for a lectureship. And you?'

'Haven't thought much about it either, but the Commodore said the civil service would have me like a shot if I cared to stay on.'

But even as she was speaking, there came a muffled crash in the distance. The windows rattled and soot came cascading down the chimney.

There had been no serious air raids for two or three years, but one could still hear explosions from time to time as demolition men coped with the damage left by the blitz, and as we had heard no air raid warning, we presumed this was a benign explosion. Then came another, and a third, each louder than the one before.

Sarah, who had lived through a good part of the London blitz, said that once one woke up in the morning and found oneself in one piece, one learned to take everything else in one's stride. The bombers usually came at night, one was given due warning of their approach, and one could get through one's work without too much disturbance.

'You learned to live with it, like you learn to live with an ache in the bones,' she said.

This new blitz was more insidious. It was inflicted by unmanned bombers, or doodle-bugs, as we came to call them, as if they were some minor irritant, and they came at great speed, without warning, at any time of the day or night, and landed with devastating effect. One could hear their droning overhead and then, as their engines cut out, one had about ten seconds to dash for shelter.

One day I was crossing Trafalgar Square. I must have been deeply preoccupied, for I could hear nothing overhead, when suddenly, everyone about me fell flat on his face, and the square looked like a vast, open-air Moslem prayer-meeting. And before I too could prostrate myself, there came an almighty blast and I was knocked from my feet. When I rose I could see a large cloud rising at the back of the Houses of Parliament and presumed that the bomb had fallen on Pimlico.

I was frankly terrified and was both pained and surprised by my own reaction. When I was in the army, I yearned for the chance of active service, but then I suppose I had thought of war in classical terms, with two lines facing one another in armed combat, and the enemy seen and identifiable. Here one felt helpless. The enemy was unseen and unannounced, and death could come out of the skies at any time of the day or night, but because everyone lived with the same danger, and the same imminence of death, relationships became more intimate and intense, and one almost felt one was cheating the enemy by any happiness one might extract from the situation. Sarah forgot about her piano, and her passion for hot water, and moved all her belongings to my flat.

Although more than a month had passed since Kleindorf vanished, she had not yet been found alternative work, but the Commodore, who looked upon her with a fatherly eye, had assured her that she would not be posted outside the London area, so that there was no threat to our relationship.

We went away frequently at weekends and usually stayed with my sister, partly because it was economic to do so, and partly because Sunny was now in Europe and she was in need of company. Both she and Sarah had reservations about each other, but they liked each other immensely, and they sometimes made me feel like an intruder. Once when we were alone together, Sosh said to me: 'The more I get to know her, the more I'm impressed with her. In fact there's so much to her – '

'That you wonder what she sees in me.'

'I wasn't going to say that, but you know the cynic I am. She really does seem to be too good to be true, and I wonder if she has something to hide.'

'Such as what? A husband? Illegitimate children? Madness in the family?'

'Perhaps all three. She's obviously from an old family, and the older the family, the more skeletons in the cupboard. Have you actually proposed to her, or anything like that?'

I doubt if the word marriage had so much as entered our

conversation, but whenever we discussed plans each presumed the involvement of the other. To all intents and purposes we were married, and if there were any social occasions to attend, we were always invited together, and yet, I at no time contemplated the possibility of taking her up to Manchester, nor did she ever suggest a visit to her parents, who lived no great distance away in Peterborough. We were both aware of difficulties ahead, but she was the first to broach them.

She had mentioned her family intermittently. I knew that she had two brothers in the armed forces and that her father had been decorated for gallantry in the first world war. He was a railwayman who had worked his way up through the company to a position on the board. Her mother was from an old county family, and she had met and married her father while he was still a ticket-collector and had, as a result, been virtually disowned by her parents. Her father, she told me, was a self-made man, liberal-minded in many respects, but he did not like Jews.

'If we marry,' she said, 'it'll be almost a matter of history repeating itself.'

She used the word 'marry' without self-consciousness.

'But what have your parents got against Jews?'

'In the case of mother, nothing, but she's too gentle and sweet to challenge father's attitudes. In the case of father, blind prejudice.'

'Perhaps he can't forgive us for killing Christ.'

'That's about the only thing he can forgive, because he's anti-religious. Perhaps he can't forgive the Jews for having given birth to Christ in the first place. To be honest, I've never discussed it seriously with him, if only because I never took it seriously until I met you. Would you like to meet him?'

'I suppose I'll have to sooner or later, but how do you yourself feel about it?'

'You should know that by now. I hardly met any Jews before I came to London. Since then I've hardly met anyone else. That's why the Commodore and I are such close friends. We feel outnumbered.'

It was then that I raised the problem of my family, but it was clear that she had already been briefed – after a fashion –

by my sister.

'I gather your father's a religious bigot,' she said.

'Bigot, probably; religious, I'm not so sure. He's different things at different times, depending on what he's heard on the radio, how he slept, and what he had for lunch, but he's invested a great deal of hope in me, and he would not be too happy if his son, his only son, were to marry a *shiksha*, the daughter of a railwayman.'

'But the granddaughter of a Baronet.'

'Are you?'

'He has nothing to do with us, and we have nothing to do with him, and the title is Irish, but a Baronet he undoubtedly is.'

'That actually would make a difference, for snobbery is the one consistent element in his make-up.'

'What about yourself? Sosh says you were nearly a Rabbi.'

'God forbid! I certainly spent a great deal of my free time in synagogue and was fairly religious, not out of any settled pattern of convictions, but because that's what I always was, and I didn't realize what a burden it was until I joined the army. I can't say I've shrugged it all off for good, for it surfaced again when I became an acolyte to an army chaplain, and it flourishes in a certain defined environment, but it's been quiescent since.'

'Sounds a little like father's cynical malaria. Supposing it should surface again?'

'We'll have to learn to cope with it.'

We decided to tackle her family first because they were the nearest and because, she felt, they posed less of a problem, though when we were seated in the train she felt the need to unburden herself of a dark secret.

'I'd better warn you,' she said, 'that my people are fairly well off and live in rather grand style.'

'Is that something to be ashamed of?'

'In a way it is, especially in wartime, but it's been a source of embarrassment to me all my life. It wasn't so bad at school, because many of my friends had grand homes – much grander than ours – with lots of servants, but it was an embarrassment at University, and it's been an embarrassment since. It's one of the reasons I haven't taken you home until now. Father's a socialist by conviction, but conservative in habit, and he hasn't let the war interfere with his ways. Our servants are old and decrepit, so they've been able to stay, and we grow most of our food, so we're hardly short of anything. It is quite shameful in some ways, but, as mother put it, he nearly lost his life in the last war, so he's entitled to live it up in this one.'

The house, a red-brick mansion just outside Peterborough, standing in its own spacious grounds, was indeed grand, much grander than *chez* Rodgers in its prime.

'Not bad for a railwayman,' I said.

'Mother was left money by various childless uncles and aunts, if you must know,' she said. 'She was everybody's favourite.'

I could understand why as soon as I met her. She was a tall, thin woman with a toothy, or rather, gummy, smile, high cheek-bones and grey hair, and she put me at ease the moment I arrived.

'I'm glad you were able to come. Sarah hardly brings anyone home – I think she's ashamed of us – and the boys are out of the country, and so we rarely see a civilized face. We don't see all that many uncivilized ones either, for that matter. Jack, that's my husband – has Sarah warned you about him? I shouldn't imagine she has, otherwise you wouldn't have come – has strong opinions on almost everything, and if you're only going to be here a short time, you may find it best to agree with everything he says. Not that he turns violent if one contradicts him. Wouldn't be so bad if he did, but if he is contradicted, he goes on to support his argument with a great volume of facts which may or may not be correct, but which are very, very boring.' All of which made him sound so much like my own father, that I looked forward to meeting him.

Nothing she or Sarah said, however, prepared me for the man himself. He was a giant, well over six foot tall, with shoulders to match, and the moment he strode in holding out a great hand in greeting, I felt like a mouse in the presence of a mountain.

I had managed to overcome my obsession with size to the extent that even my sister no longer noticed it. Sarah was only slightly taller than me, and was always careful to wear flat shoes in my company. Her mother was a good bit taller, but that didn't worry me. But her father! Short as I was, I felt myself getting shorter under his very gaze, and wishing that I could vanish altogether. The loftiness of the rooms didn't help either.

They obviously noticed my discomfiture and tried to make me feel at ease, and I tried to rally my spirits with drink, but got drunk without feeling merry and sleepy without feeling relaxed. Sarah held my hand throughout, wiped my lapel when I spilt wine on it, and my tie when I spilt soup on it and my brow when I began to perspire.

'Are you all right darling,' she kept saying, 'would you like to lie down for a bit?'

Faces became distorted, voices incoherent, or was that me talking incoherently? She eventually put me to bed in a semi-comatose state.

We left the next day.

We could not talk much in the train because it was very crowded, and in any case we did not have all that much to say.

'I'm sorry, I rather disgraced myself.'

'Hardly that, but I will admit that you were not at your scintillating best. Perhaps you shouldn't drink so much.'

There was a tartness in her voice I had never noticed before.

When we got to King's Cross she said she was going on to south London.

'I haven't practised the piano for months. I've been getting rusty. Mother remarked on it.'

I didn't try to persuade her otherwise. If anything, I was relieved.

CHAPTER ELEVEN

I woke after a restless night feeling it had all been a dream.

How else could one explain it? We had travelled up to Peterborough, lovers, holding hands, laughing, joking, discussing plans. We were almost man and wife. We returned strangers, and yet nothing had happened to explain the change.

I had been warmly received and regally entertained, and if I had drunk too much – which I had – it was not the first time Sarah had seen me in my cups and, as far as I recalled, nothing had been said by me to which anyone could have taken exception. Her father, like most self-made men (and not a few self-unmade men) was opinionated and a bit full of himself, but I had been prepared for that, and I might even have found it endearing, for it should have suggested that he was not quite the giant he looked, but I could not shake off my sense of inadequacy. I had declined not only in my own eyes, but – or so I felt – in those of Sarah, for if her voice was sympathetic and even loving, she looked puzzled, pained, reproachful, as well she might, for I felt that I had been abandoned by my usual self. The more I thought about it the more confused I became.

Sarah must have felt the same, for she rang me a little later. 'How did you sleep?'

'Not very well. And you?'

'Hardly at all. A lot of things kept going through my mind. We'd better talk, hadn't we?'

She arrived a few hours later and the moment she stepped over the threshold I knew that it was all over for, to use a Biblical expression which has somehow lingered in my mind, her face 'was not towards me as before'.

We kissed, we talked, we ate, we made love – or tried to –

we bathed together and tried again (rather more successfully), and talked once more, but we were both aware that the soul had gone out of our relationship.

'I think it's what your sister calls your "kosher streak",' she said. 'You're a rational man and you thought once you had shaken off your religious beliefs, there was no reason why your background should stand in the way of our relationship, and I felt the same, but once you set foot in our house, your nerve failed and you became quite literally a different person, as if you had reverted to an earlier self. I couldn't understand what had happened. I think you'll agree that my parents went out of their way to be nice to you – '

'They were absolutely charming.'

'And yet you looked as if you wanted to run away, and I almost wished you had, for I kept holding your hand and looking into your face, and I felt I was looking at a stranger.'

'There may be a simpler explanation,' I said. 'I've never told you this, but I used to be very self-conscious about my height – '

'Do you think I don't know? Why do you think I've been wearing flat shoes all these months? I hate flat shoes, I've never looked good in them. What's your height got to do with it?'

'Let me finish. The moment your father appeared with his arm extended, all the self-confidence went out of me. He's a giant – '

'So what should I do? Cut off his legs?'

'You know, you're beginning to sound Jewish.'

'But I don't see what you're getting at. The Commodore's a large man, does he make you feel small?'

'Yes, but it's a contained largeness. Your father's overwhelming. Everything about him is large, his voice, his manner. He seemed to fill the house.'

She shook her head.

'I'm sorry, it doesn't make sense. You thought you had your kosher streak under control, whereas in fact it has you under control. That doesn't sound rational either, but I can see no other explanation.'

We were both silent for a while after that, each wrapped up in our own thoughts. I had not switched the light on and it was so quiet one could almost hear the dusk settle over the city.

'I shall miss this room,' she said, 'and I shall miss the view, especially the towers and turrets of St Pancras station on a misty morning. I shall even miss the musty smell.'

'But you won't miss me.'

'I shall miss you most of all, dear Sammy,' and putting her arms round me, she broke down.

'This is absurd,' I said.

'I know it is, but there's nothing we can do about it,' and still sobbing, she pulled her case from under the bed and began to pack.

She was not in the office the next day and the Commodore told me she was on leave. He looked at me searchingly as he gave me the information, hoping that I might have something to say, but I did not at that moment feel like talking at all. I wondered if she had told him anything, for he always had a mildly sad air about him even at convivial moments, and he seemed infinitely sadder that morning. I was more forthcoming when we met for drinks after work and told him our relationship was over.

'I thought it must have been something like that,' he said, 'for it's not like her to ask for leave at short notice. Poor girl, things never do seem to work out for her, but then you see she's a blue stocking and upper class, and the two don't mix.'

A few weeks later, she was transferred to the Admiralty and moved to Cheltenham.

When I told Sosh what had happened, she was incredulous.

'I'm sorry, but people's minds, hearts, bowels, or balls if you prefer, just don't work like that. You can't build up a relationship over months, live together virtually as husband and wife, and suddenly find yourself strangers in the course of an evening for no reason at all. She says you got cold feet, but if you ask me, it was the other way about, for as soon as she saw you under her own roof, the reality of the situation suddenly came home to her. Here she was, a baronet's granddaughter, an heiress, in a stately home, sitting at table with this jumped-up little Jew-boy from nowhere, who wasn't even born in this country. Oh the whole thing was nice enough for an office affair and dirty weekends. It helped to see one through the war, and what with doodle-bugs falling all around, and death in the air, it must have made those snatched moments of passion seem all the more passionate, but once she was back with her own family, she realized that you didn't really belong to the same world. I can imagine how her mind worked. What'll happen to the children? He'll probably want the little bastards circumcised, and drag them to synagogue, and top them up on Christian blood on Passover. No ham and eggs for breakfast, not even after the end of rationing, no bacon and sausages, no gammon steak, no pork chops. And then there's his wretched family, foreigners all, and cousins, no doubt, who'll descend over the Jewish holidays to make sure that everything's nice and kosher, and at Christmas to boot. Didn't she say her father was an anti-semite?'

'He didn't behave like one.'

'No English anti-semite ever does. She probably saw you, and her life ahead, through her father's eyes. She asked me a lot of questions about Judaism, you know, and how you felt about it, and I was perfectly frank – I always am.'

'You're more than frank, you're defamatory.'

'Are you trying to tell me your upbringing means nothing to you? You practically lived in the synagogue when you were a boy.'

'You also had a kosher upbringing, and it seems to have made no lasting impression on you.'

'No, but I made damn sure it didn't. I fought it, you revelled in it, and it left you with an ineradicable kosher streak. I told her that.'

'I know, but it didn't worry her in the least.'

'Not until she was under her own roof, when it suddenly hit her.'

'You don't understand the whole situation. She was deeply distressed.'

'She would be, people always are when reality catches up on them. She's thirty, or over, obviously wants to marry and have children before it gets tricky, and she talked herself into believing that you were the man. And you could have been. You're attractive and obviously bright, you're highly regarded by your superiors, and you're someone who'll get somewhere. You'll do, she thought, and you did – until she brought you home. If you had only kept your parents out of it, you might have lived happily ever after, but it's too late now. I'm sorry it's over, deeply sorry, because I liked her very much, and I think she liked me.'

'Perhaps you should have married each other.'

The conversation left me feeling slightly disturbed, for although I undoubtedly did have a kosher streak, I wondered in what terms Sosh had described it, for given the strength of her imagination, and her capacity for exaggeration, she might have depicted me as a religious fanatic and put the fear of God into the poor girl.

Nor did I feel that she was a totally disinterested party. She may have been perfectly happy to accommodate us for a dirty weekend, but marriage was another matter, for in spite of her protestations of affection for Sarah, I could not overlook the glint of joy in her eyes when I told her it was all over.

But over it was and, whatever the cause, there was no point in engaging in endless post-mortems, and though it wasn't easy I tried to put it out of my mind. My health declined and, for the first time since I had outgrown childhood ailments, I fell ill. I found it difficult to sleep or to eat, I lost weight, couldn't concentrate and became prone to violent headaches.

I tried to continue with my work as usual, but it became impossible and, on the insistence of the Commodore, I went to see the MO. He examined me in some detail and sent me to Charing Cross Hospital for a further examination. They could find nothing organically wrong with me, but I was given a letter to an eye specialist, a Lt Col. Bannerman.

My heart leapt at the very sound of the name, for I presumed he must be Emma's husband. She had mentioned he was in Egypt, but that was more than a year ago. It says something for my state of dejection that the sound of his name was almost a cure in itself. I straightened up, my movements became less leaden, my appetite improved. I had something to look forward to, and did so with such anticipation, that one might have thought that I was about to have a passionate encounter with the woman herself, rather than a professional appointment with her husband.

But when I was ushered into his presence my spirits

sagged, for he was a bent, elderly figure with grey hair, shaggy eyebrows, thick glasses and a flushed face. He could have been a relative, or another Bannerman, but I could not imagine that he could be her husband.

He beckoned to me to sit down while he pored over an open file on his desk and then, still without a word, shone a strong light into my face while he examined my eyes. His breath reeked of whisky.

'Now what's your trouble?' he demanded, at which I sat up, for there was no mistaking his Scottish accent.

'Are you from Glasgow?' I asked.

'I ask the questions round here,' he snarled. 'Now what's your trouble?'

'I'm not too sure myself.'

'Then what are you doing here?'

'I was sent here.'

'Nothing wrong with your eyes, though you could probably do with a new pair of specs.'

He gave me an eye test, and then as he sat down to write the prescription, I felt emboldened to try again. 'Are you from Glasgow?'

'Ah heard you the furst time.'

'I used to know a Mrs Bannerman in Glasgow.'

'Aye, and you're not the only one. Did she tweak your prick?'

'Did she do what?'

'Tweak your prick,' he roared. 'It's not your eyes that want testing, it's your ears.'

'We can't be talking about the same Mrs Bannerman.'

'A young woman with a wee boy and big tits?'

'Y-yes, that does sound like her.'

'Her husband's in the army?'

'Yes.'

'An eye specialist?'

'I believe so.'

'It's her all right. So did she, or didn't she?'

'Didn't she what?'

'Tweak your prick?'

'I'm afraid not.'

'Well, better luck next time.'

I emerged in a daze. What was an attractive young woman like her doing with a cantankerous old man like him? Was she as promiscuous as he suggested, and if she was, why did he treat it in such a matter-of-fact way? He seemed almost to revel in it. It then, however, occurred to me that his accent was so thick I may have misunderstood him and, after some hesitation, I put my head round the door. He was dictating to a secretary and he glowered at me with the gravest displeasure.

'What is it now?'

His eyebrows alone were enough to repel an army, but I held my ground.

'Do you think you can spare me a minute?'

'No, ah can't.'

'It's about Mrs Bannerman.'

'What about her?'

'It's private.'

'I'll bet it is.'

I looked uneasily at his secretary.

'You needn't worry about her, she's heard it all before. Now what is it, and be quick about it, ah haven't got all day.'

'It may be none of my business, but aren't you troubled by her conduct?'

'Whose conduct?'

'Mrs Bannerman's.'

'Ah would be if she was mah wife, but as she's mah daughter-in-law, ah don't give a fuck.'

As I closed the door, he shouted after me: 'Try her again, you'll get there yet – they all do.'

That Christmas was the most desolate of my life.

A week in the bosom of my family was a dispiriting experience at the best of times, and this was the worst of times, for after five years of hostilities, war weariness had set in with a vengeance, and one could almost feel it on one's lungs, like a gritty fog.

In the summer everyone was confident that war would be over by Christmas. Now Christmas was upon us, and there was no end in sight yet. The Americans had been checked in the Ardennes. The headlong advance of the Russians had slowed down. Italy was not yet completely liberated. There was civil war in Greece, and whole fleets were being sent to the bottom of the sea, so that shortages were acute, and possibly because the actual outcome of the war was no longer in doubt, people allowed themselves to luxuriate in a certain amount of despondency, and our home was no exception, though it did, at least, display the virtue of changelessness. Father still spent most of his free time bent over the radio, mother still spent hers darning socks, though there was no longer a cheerful fire in the grate – instead there was some dark incombustible matter which filled the room with smoke, but gave no warmth.

Father's first words of greeting as I stepped over the threshold were: 'You a Captain yet? Kreiger's boy, the one with the funny teeth's a Captain, with a fine brown belt, and a little cane.'

'Sunny's a Captain, you should be satisfied with that,' said mother.

'But Sunny's a lawyer, and he looks an officer, but young Kreiger looks like his father, a tailor. You'd think, seeing he's a Captain, that he would at least have his teeth straightened. That's one thing you've got to say for the Americans, teeth like pianos, even the privates.' And he turned to me: 'You should emigrate to America when the war's over.'

'My teeth are all right.'

'Nothing to do with teeth. It's the country of the future.'

It was a theme to which he was to return at frequent intervals. Sunny had been home on leave recently and had told them that he hoped to stay on in England after the war.

'Mad,' said father.

'Why mad?' asked mother.

'If you knew what I know, you'd know he was mad.'

'So what do you know?'

'What don't I know? In Poland they used to tell me England was a land of gentlemen. Maybe it was, but I can tell you what it is now – a land of thieves. All right, you have thieves everywhere, and they'll take money, jewellery, valuables, but here they steal things because they're there. Where I work – I shouldn't be telling you this, because it's all secret – '

'Walls have ears,' I said.

'You wouldn't believe this, but in the canteen they make

off with the salt-cellars, mustard-pots, ashtrays, knives and forks, cups and saucers, pots and pans – before they've even been washed. I said to the manager, they'd make off with the chip-fryer if it wasn't screwed down. And what happens? They make off with the chip-fryer. And that's while there's still a war on. When the war's over they'll be making off with whole factories. A land of thieves. If I was a younger man I'd emigrate to America myself.'

'Have they no thieves in America?' asked mother.

'Maybe, but there's more to steal. But here? Anything Hitler hasn't destroyed is being knocked off.'

Mother put down one pair of socks and picked up another. Where, I wondered, did she find all those socks to darn? One would think father was a centipede, or that she was sub-contracting for a sock-darning company. She seemed to have become noticeably older and thinner since I last saw her, and more strained. She could hardly have been more than fifty but already had something of the appearance and bearing of a little old lady. I also noticed that she went to bed rather earlier than she used to.

'Easiest way to keep warm,' father explained. 'Coal you can't get, and the stuff you do get isn't coal and doesn't burn.' He also mentioned a recent visit to Sosh which had left them exhausted.

'Three changes we had to make, which isn't so terrible, but there was an hour's wait at each change, and when we did get on, the trains were packed. She had to stand half the way. She would have had to stand the whole way, if I hadn't given her my seat. I said to Soshanna, now that Sunny's in France, or wherever he is, why don't you come and stay with us in Manchester? You'll save on heating, if nothing else, but you know your sister.'

It later emerged that mother went to bed early because she could not take the late-night news bulletins in Russian and Polish.

Reports about the extermination of European Jewry had been circulating for some two years now, but one either had a limited ability to absorb such horrors, or one's faith in human nature made it difficult to believe them.

Father was from a small family and had very few relatives

left in Poland, but mother had a great many. She no longer allowed herself to hope that her elderly parents could be alive, but she also had brothers, nephews, nieces, uncles, aunts, cousins, some fifty souls in all, and she refused to believe that they had all been done to death.

'I started saying *kaddish* for everybody I knew, years ago,' father said, 'but you know your mother. She's been asking everybody, and writing to everybody and hearing from nobody, which is why she looks the way she looks.'

I was rather upset that she had not raised the matter with me, as if I was too tender a soul to be burdened with such things.

'What's the point?' she said. 'What could you do that I haven't done?'

As soon as I got back to London I wrote to Holtzhacker asking for an introduction to Mac or, if he was out of the country, to a Polish officer of equal rank. A few weeks later I got a reply from Fr Urbansky to say that Holtzhacker had last been seen in Naples on May 12th and that nothing had been heard of him since, and that Mac was recuperating from an operation in the Hammersmith hospital. The following day he phoned to say that he had spoken to Mac and that he would be happy to see me.

He looked anything but happy, poor man, sitting up in bed, pale faced and gaunt, his moustache white, his teeth black, his gums swollen and his head shaking.

He put on his glasses when I entered and scrutinized me without recognition. My name didn't mean anything to him either, but when I mentioned Holtzhacker (or rather, Gilchrist), something like a smile lit up his glasses.

'He's vanished you know. But he'll turn up. The Gilchrists of this world always do. Not in the least like any priest I've ever met, that's why I liked him. So you were his assistant, yes, of course, I remember you very well.'

Fr Urbansky had already told him the reason for my visit, and he shook his head dolefully.

'I can offer you no hope, none whatever. I have no more hope for Polish Jewry than for Poland itself. The whole place is a charnel-house.'

'But surely there must be some survivors. There were over three million Jews in Poland.'

'Where do your people come from?'

'A small place near Bydgoszcz.'

'Ha, charming town. I know it well. Did you people call it Bydgoszcz? I ask, because most Jews called it Bomberg, the German name. Easier to pronounce, I suppose.'

'And infinitely easier to spell.'

'Indeed.'

'Father always called it Bydgoszcz.'

'Did you speak Polish at home?'

'Yiddish mostly, though he turned to English as soon as he could.'

'Odd place Bydgoszcz. As you know, the Prussians annexed western Poland in the eighteenth century. The Jews, on the whole, were happier with the arrangement than the Poles, for they've always had an affinity for German culture. Even Yiddish is largely German. In the Hapsburg Empire, where I grew up, the Jews were the main carriers and propagators of German language and culture. If Hitler had not taken on the Jews, they would have been amongst his staunchest allies.'

'But weren't the Jews the mainstay of the left-wing movements in central Europe?'

'Not only in central Europe, almost everywhere. I had a colleague who used to refer to the Comintern as the Sanhedrin, but by the thirties the Jewish bourgeoisie were recoiling from their own radicals. They would have rallied round Hitler if he had let them. We had a Jewish neighbour, a wealthy landowner, a generous and cultured man. He opened a school for the children of his tenants, and paid for it out of his own pocket, but though his tenants were Polish, the teaching was German. When Bydgoszcz returned to Poland in 1918, most of the Jews opted to return to Germany. I suppose they regarded it as a golden land, poor souls. There was a time when they regarded Poland as a golden land. It was a magnet for Jews everywhere, and they flourished nowhere as they did in Poland. And if things went wrong, as I'm afraid they did, could it have been entirely the fault of the Poles? Perhaps we were too much alike, both stubborn, both unruly, both with long memories, both burdened with a great past, but our greatness is more recent, and perhaps more burdensome. We were an empire in the sixteenth century, the arbiters of Europe and the saviours of Christendom in the seventeenth. We are slaves now.'

He was lost in thought for a moment, then looked up and smiled apologetically. 'I'm sorry, you didn't come here for a seminar in Polish history. People with long memories are terrible bores. You want my help but, as you see, I'm helpless. Look at me, and you can see Poland, partly consumed now, wholly consumed soon. You people will rise again, it is your fate: we shall be betrayed again, it is ours.'

Tears welled up in his eyes, and began to trickle down his cheeks. 'Forgive me,' he said, 'I'm an old man and my functions are out of control.'

He held out his hand and I clasped it in both mine. It was cold and clammy, like the hand of a corpse.

CHAPTER TWELVE

In the course of our memorable journey up to Peterborough, Sarah and I had mapped out our joint future in considerable detail. We decided, as a start, that we both liked London and wished to remain there. Sarah was more or less assured of a job in the permanent civil service by the Commodore, and I decided to try and find a teaching job in one of the colleges of London University.

When I returned from Peterborough, I had to think again and began to re-examine the possibility of going on to Cambridge for a higher degree. Most of my colleagues were Cambridge men and, as one of them put it, one is not really taken seriously as a mathematician until one has Cantab. after one's name.

While I was thus dithering one evening in the flat, I received an unexpected visitor. He entered, a man in black, asked how I was, noted that I had lost weight, then stood for a time admiring the view of the spires of St Pancras station from my window.

He obviously knew me and, as obviously, took it that I knew him, which I did, but I could not put a name to his face, or an occasion to our last meeting. It was only when he took off his black homburg and put on a black skull-cap that I recognized the Rev. Pollock from Glasgow.

I offered him a drink.

'No, no, no. This is not a social call and, as I have to catch a train, I had better get straight to the point. Do you remember Emma Bannerman? I'm sure you must. You were guests together at my Passover table nearly two years ago, and once encountered, she is not easily forgotten.'

'What about her?'

'She's getting divorced.'

'I'm sorry to hear that.'

'Are you really? Come now, Mr Hoch – or may I call you Samuel?'

'You may call me Sammy.'

'We are men of the world, even though my dress may suggest otherwise. You fed on the sight of her to the exclusion of the wine, the matzoth, the chicken-soup, the *kneidlech*, the chicken itself, the compote. My wife was upset. She thought you disliked her cooking, but I explained that you had been feasting on another dish.'

'I found her attractive, if that's what you mean, but who wouldn't?'

'Exactly, but she has, unfortunately, fallen out with her husband. He is suing for divorce, and if she should contest it, a lot of things would come out which would reflect badly on the good name of a community which I have had the honour to serve for the past twenty years.'

'But forgive me, Reverend, what has all this to do with me? Is he citing me as a co-respondent?'

'Heaven forbid. I have known Emma since she was a child. She is a woman who needs a husband and has a child who needs a father, and if there was a husband and father immediately in prospect, she could, I think, be persuaded to leave the divorce uncontested.'

'And you want me to be the prospective husband and father.'

'Exactly.'

'Why me?'

'Why not?'

'How do you know she would want me?'

'I know because I make it my business to know. Apart from everything else, I am, so to speak, her father confessor.'

'And she confessed to a passion for me?'

'Surely you will not have me betray the secrets of the confessional.'

'And what makes you so sure I would want her?'

'I am not sure, but I would be surprised if you didn't.'

'Reverend Pollock, with respect, you don't know the first thing about me.'

'Oh but I do, and the second thing, and the third. You see I was a good friend of your good friend Rabbi Gilchrist, alias Holtzhacker and, if it comes to that, I know a few things about your good friend Rabbi Holtzhacker, alias Gilchrist.'

'He's vanished, you know.'

'So I understand, and with good cause, but that's beside the point. We are talking about an attractive young woman, intelligent, vivacious, well set up, with her own house and a bit of private money, and more than a bit to come when her mother goes.'

The whole idea, bizarre as it was, did not seem entirely implausible to me, until he mentioned her mother, at which the rather attractive picture which had been forming in my imagination, suddenly popped!

'Her mother?'

'She does have a mother, and I would not be frank if I suggested that she was but a sweet old dear. Sweet she isn't, and dear she isn't, but old she is. She married late, had her child late, and she's in failing health. In other words, she's one of those problems which will solve themselves with time.'

'In case I misunderstood you, Reverend, shall we try and recap. You are anxious to protect the good name of your community and to that end you want me, a casual acquaintance, to marry a woman with a murky past – '

'Heaven forbid! What makes you say that?'

'If her past isn't murky, why are you afraid of nasty revelations?'

'You obviously don't know much about human nature, and even less about divorce courts. She is, as I said, a very attractive young woman, and attractive young women, as, indeed, attractive old ones, are presumed guilty until they are found innocent. Now I wouldn't swear that she is, in fact, a complete innocent. She has certainly been almost wilfully indiscreet and, as a result, all sorts of rumours have been billowing round her like smoke, which will no doubt be served up as hard fact if the case is contested. Divorces can bring out the worst in the most amiable people. Every fault is exaggerated, every foible enlarged, every virtue is overlooked, all the mitigating circumstances are dismissed, and everything is painted in the harshest and blackest colours. It would be a calamity.'

'How old is she?'

'About twenty-five, twenty-six maybe. She married young, which is part of the trouble. She's a few years older than you, but you strike me as a young man old for his years.'

'I'm not sure if I regard that as a compliment.'

'As you know, us Jews have always associated years with wisdom.'

'So she is about twenty-five, with an obstreperous child, and an impossible mother – '

'But, as I said, an old one.'

'I've met the mother, you know, and I suspect she would outlive us all, if only for spite.'

'Sammy, she's an ailing woman.'

'It's the ailing members of a family who send the healthy ones to an early grave. To be perfectly frank, Reverend Pollock, I have heard things about Mrs Bannerman which make me doubt if I would accept your proposition even if she was on her own.'

'I have never suggested she was perfectly innocent.'

'No one is perfectly innocent, but there are degrees of imperfection. I'm not talking about mere tittle-tattle. I have heard things about her which I daren't repeat in the presence of a clergyman, and from someone who is in a position to know.'

'One of her sisters-in-law, no doubt.'

'No, but you're getting warm.'

'Well who was it?'

'Her father-in-law'

'Isaac Bannerman? Is he still alive? I thought the old scoundrel had drunk himself to death.'

'He's a very eminent physician.'

'A brilliant man, but mad, completely mad. He opposed the marriage from the beginning, on purely snobbish grounds, and was convinced that his son was seduced into it. I will admit that the infant was born a month or two earlier than it should have been, but the son was no innocent himself. He knew what he was doing and what he had done, and even tried to have it undone, but on second thoughts they decided to go through with it.'

'A shot-gun wedding.'

'That's how his family thought of it, and they boycotted the ceremony, but I've married more couples than you've had hot dinners, and many's the time that I've looked at the pair under the *chupah* and asked myself, what have they done to me that I should be doing this to them, for I can see nothing but misfortune ahead. But I can tell a likely pair when I see one, with happy prospects and, but for the war, those two would have been happily married to this day, and, even with the war and the separations, there would have been no trouble, but for the poison which his two sisters have poured into his ear. So there you have the whole story. All right, she has her faults and drawbacks, but I assure you that it would never have occurred to me to put this idea to you, if I had not been convinced that you'd be doing yourself a good turn. In any case I am not asking you to compromise yourself in any way. All I want you to do is to meet her again.'

I was tempted to follow that up with, 'Don't know where, don't know when, but I know we'll meet again some sunny day,' but I didn't want to upset him, for he was beginning to look slightly distressed.

'I will have that drink after all,' he said hoarsely. 'Whisky if you have it.'

I had a little, and he finished the little I had.

'I think I may have tackled this the wrong way. The trouble is, I'm too honest and too direct, which is a dangerous failing in a clergyman. Look, Emma will be in London for a wedding next week, and I want you to do me a personal favour and go along to that wedding, nothing more.'

'Which wedding? What wedding? I don't know anyone who's getting married.'

'That's beside the point. I'll get you an invitation. In fact I've got one right here, but when you see her you mustn't mention the divorce, or that you saw me, or that we talked, or anything like that. In fact I want you to treat this whole visit as if it hasn't happened.'

He handed me the invitation. It was large and gilt-edged and looked garishly opulent. The names meant nothing to me.

'Supposing she asks what I'm doing there?'

'Tell her you're a cousin, which you probably are. They're

a vast family and related to everyone. It's a Sunday afternoon, so you can't even say you're busy. Will you go?'

The whole idea was so bizarre, and the possibilities so intriguing, that I could hardly refuse.

He almost danced with joy, and shook my hand vigorously.

'You'll bless this day,' he said. 'I promise you.'

The wedding was in a north-west London synagogue and as I was approaching the entrance, a taxi pulled up and a pair of shapely legs emerged, and I knew whose they were even before the rest of her appeared. When she turned and saw me, she let out a small scream and dropped her handbag.

'It's not you, is it?'

'I sincerely hope it is.'

'But that bowler hat.'

I took it off. 'Is that better?'

'Very much better. Why didn't you write?'

'Write?'

'Letters – "my dearest Emma" – that sort of thing. I like reading them.'

'Would you have answered?'

'Probably not, but that's beside the point. I was sure you would, and was disappointed when you didn't.'

It was February, but uncommonly mild for the time of the year, and sunny, and we talked for so long that we missed the better part of the marriage service which, however, went on so long that I was sorry we had not missed it all. The huge synagogue was packed, with women sitting on one side of the building, and men on the other.

The reception was in an adjoining hall and in the crush which ensued, I lost sight of Emma, and then as I was looking round for her, I suddenly felt a heavy hand on my shoulder. I stiffened. My game was up.

I turned my head slowly, expecting the outraged father of the bride, and found myself facing a small, plump, sandy-haired figure with thick glasses.

'I thought it was you,' he said. 'How are you?'

I searched his unlovely features for some detail which might activate a spring in my memory. There was none, but I was still not sure whether this was a case of mistaken identity on his part, or a lapse of memory on mine.

'Not too bad at all,' I said finally.

'You've lost weight.'

'I've been ill.'

'You too? You have been going through a hard time of it in one way or another, haven't you?' (The mistake was obviously his, but it was by now too late to do anything about it.)

'How's your mother?'

'Fine.'

'Is she?'

'Shouldn't she be?'

'Well to be honest, I was afraid to ask because I heard it was touch and go, but then I reckoned it couldn't be that bad if you're here. So she's pulled through, has she?'

'Oh yes, she's well on the mend.'

'Shows you, doesn't it? My old woman wasn't so lucky, as you know. The stone-setting's a week on Sunday, if you can make it, at Edmonton.' He looked around him and lowered his voice. 'Hear anything from Ruby?'

'Ruby?'

'Your brother. I know you don't like talking about him, but you can tell him I'm on his side. I'd have done the same in his position. More sinned against than sinning, is Ruby.'

All the time he was talking I was turning my head this way and that, looking for Emma, and he remarked upon my inattention.

'I know Ruby's a sore point with you and your family, but we're none of us angels, are we? Not even you for that matter. You wasn't quite the gentleman you think you are when it came to my sister, was you? Don't think I don't know, because she told me everything, and if it wasn't for the fact that I thought your mother was dying, I'd have had it out with you there and then.' He raised his voice. 'Ruby's worth ten of you – '

At which I dived into the crowd, as a desperate man might dive into a boiling cauldron, cut through the mass of bodies and legs, and surfaced to find her standing in front of me. I immediately grabbed her by the hand, pulled her from the hall, and out into the street.

'What the hell are you doing?'

'I can't stand it in there. Can't we go for a drink somewhere?'

'What do you think they're serving in there, hemlock?'

'But it's impossible to move or to talk. Wouldn't you like to come to my place?'

'Come into my parlour, said the spider to the fly. Let's go to my hotel, we can have tea in the lounge.'

In the taxi I apologized. 'I'm sorry for grabbing you like that. I suppose I hate crowds.'

'I may like crowds for all you know – not that I do.'

'Did you come down all the way from Glasgow especially?'

'Good God no, I had to be in London in any case, but what were you doing there?'

'What does anyone do at a wedding? I'm a relative.'

'Liar. You were there because you knew I'd be there. Who told you, Bollocks?'

'Who?'

'The Reverend Efrem Pollock, but that's how mother pronounces his name, and that's how he's known in the family.'

'Why Pollock?'

'Because he urged me to go in the first place. They are in fact relatives, but I went out of curiosity, to see who he might have up his sleeve. A bit like that half-blind date we had in the tea room – remember? I'm glad it was you.'

'No flies on you, are there?'

'There is on you, and it's open.'

When we got to the hotel and were having tea in the lounge, she said: 'Did he tell you I was getting divorced?'

'Are you?'

'As if you didn't know. Can I give you a piece of advice? Stick to the truth, because you haven't got the makings of a liar. It's an art, being a successful liar. You're either born with it, or you're not.'

'Are you?'

'No, but if I was you wouldn't know if I was telling the truth in the first place, so there's no point in asking.'

'How long will it take?'

'The divorce? Ages. It's so bloody complicated. We were married in Scotland, but domiciled in England and I only moved back to Glasgow when he was sent abroad, which means two sets of lawyers. That's why I'm here, and it's costing a bloody fortune.'

'Are you contesting the divorce?'

'Not if he'll be reasonable about it, but he's acting despicably. Father was a barber who started with nothing. He didn't even own the trousers he wore when he came here, but within twenty years he had a whole chain of barber shops and hairdressers and more than fifty people working for him, and he sold the lot to set him up. Bought him a house in Chelsea, and consulting rooms in Harley Street, and a large car. He thought he'd bought his way into the aristocracy, poor soul. The Bannermans – or rather the Berdichevskys – were one of the oldest Jewish families in Scotland and Neville – my husband – was not only a doctor himself, but the son of a doctor, and father could see a whole medical dynasty ahead. Well, I intend to get some of that money back, not for my own sake, you understand, but for Jeremy's.'

'Doesn't he want to make provision for his own child?'

'He denies Jeremy's his child. I wish he wasn't. It's no great start for a child to have a father like that, mean, grasping, spineless. He's been afraid to speak to me since this whole thing started, it's all being done through lawyers.'

'How did you meet him?'

'I had an accident when I was seventeen or eighteen, bit of acid in my eye, and I was sent to his father who quickly cleared up the trouble, and then became a trouble in his own right – the old goat. He insisted that I come for a check-up once a month. "Eyes like yours want watching, my girl," he said. He also explained how the different organs of the body were connected, and tried to convince me that he had to poke into every orifice to see how my eyes were doing. He didn't charge me for these extra visits, but I should have charged him. No wonder so many of the boys I knew wanted to study medicine. And then I met golden boy, his son. He'd been a brilliant student, was a brilliant doctor, and he already had the makings of a brilliant specialist, and when he proposed I couldn't see how I could refuse. His family were all against it, of course. The old man, a widower, fancied me himself, but he has four sisters, all older than him, and as possessive as four mothers. He was thirty by then, pasty faced, balding and plump, but I think they were saving him for Princess Elizabeth. They all boycotted the wedding, and did their darndest to get him back. Well, they've got him, and they can keep him.'

She looked into my eyes for a moment. 'I don't know why I'm telling you all this, seeing you haven't told me a thing about yourself.'

'There's nothing to tell, I'm afraid, but your mother might be interested to know that I'm no longer a corporal.'

I took her hand and kissed it.

'Can we go to your room?' I said.

'What are you suggesting?'

'That we go to bed.'

She tried to look shocked.

'I said I was a free woman, almost, but not an abandoned one. Besides, I only have a single room.'

'We can double up.'

'No we can't. I unpacked and changed in a great hurry and it's in a terrible mess.'

'A bit of squalor does something for the libido.'

'Not for mine, it doesn't. Besides, this is a railway hotel, and railway hotels don't approve of hanky-panky.'

And so we went to my place which I had scrubbed and cleaned in the hope of such an eventuality, and the first thing she said as she entered was: 'I've never seen such a tidy bachelor's flat. You must have a woman.'

'I don't even have a cleaning woman.'

'You tidied it all yourself?'

'All of it.'

'Can you cook as well?'

'And darn.'

'You're just the man I need. Will you marry me?'